An Audience
with an Elephant

To Bryn Rogers (1909–1968),
who read none of these

Kyrchwn Loygyr, a cheisswn greft y caffom yn ymborth
From Manawyddan, son of Llyr, *The Mabinogion*, twelth century

Let us go to England to learn a craft, that we may make a living

The Sunday Telegraph

An Audience
with an Elephant

AND OTHER ENCOUNTERS
ON THE ECCENTRIC SIDE

BYRON ROGERS

Aurum Press

First published in Great Britain
2001 by Aurum Press Ltd
25 Bedford Avenue, London WC1B 3AT

Designed and typeset in 12pt Centaur by Geoff Green

The pieces included in this book were first published in the *Sunday Telegraph*, *Daily Telegraph*, *Guardian*,
Sunday Express, London *Evening Standard*, *World of Interiors* and *Saga Magazine*.

Lines on p. 63 from *Mass for Hard Times* by R. S. Thomas, published by Bloodaxe Books, 1972,
reprinted by permission of the Estate of R. S. Thomas.

A catalogue record for this book is available from the British Library.

ISBN 1 85410 786 0

3 5 7 9 10 8 6 4
2003 2005 2004 2002

Printed in Great Britain by
MPG Books Ltd, Bodmin

Contents

Foreword

READING THESE PIECES AGAIN, I am amazed I have managed to make a living from journalism. The concerns of English papers and magazines, London news, politics and the already famous, were never mine, which will explain why only two of these pieces were suggested by editors. The rest I had to persuade them to use.

Sometimes I overdid the persuasion, as when, thinking myself no end of a wag, I got the features editor of the *Sunday Telegraph* to commission a profile of an elephant on the grounds that the animal was the most successful teenager in show business; the joke stopped when I found myself having to write 2000 words about a creature which did nothing except react to food. But the persuasion I loved. It allowed me to live on my wits, and to draw on the chicanery my ancestors practised at horse-sales. Once, banned from driving, I got the features editor of the *Guardian* to commission a series on towns, and it was only when the articles were appearing that he realised the towns were within a few miles of each other. I had been hitch-hiking between them. But then, as the editor of *Saga Magazine* spotted, just about all the travels I have ever undertaken have been in that narrow corridor of land between Northampton, where I live, and Carmarthen, where I was brought up. And why not? All human life is there.

In the *Chronicle of the Princes*, a medieval Welsh history, this entry occurs, and it is one of the most wonderful sentences ever written. 'In the year 1180 there was nothing that might be placed on record.' Never such confidence again, this was probably the last time anyone had the nerve to admit there had been no news. For what is news? It is a product like any other that now must be gathered daily, for the cameras and the papers are waiting and the ploughman with his Sony Walkman needs briefing every hour on the world's woes. Yes, but *what* is it? Ah, answering that question, to quote Larkin out of context, brings the priest and the doctor running over the fields in their long coats. News is what it was in 1180: it is the fortunes of the famous, or at least those they would like known, and the misfortunes of the rest, who have no choice in the matter.

But it has been my misfortune to live in a time when these distinctions became absolute. On the one side, forever in shadow, is the overwhelming majority of people, of interest only for their purchasing power. On the other is that tiny group on whom the spotlight rests. Television has done this, the fortunes of *Hello* magazine have been based on it, and the papers have followed, creating between them the cult of celebrity. The result is that at no time in human history have so many become mere spectators, and been so conscious of the fact.

Celebrities have existed for so long as there has been any form of organised society, but there were far fewer of them: the general, the prince, the politician, the preacher, the murderer, the hangman. And they were part of a remote world. You heard about them, you saw them deified in Staffordshire pottery, you read about them in newspapers which arrived two days late. So you had a different attitude, which occasionally they shared. When William IV became King of England he did not see why he should not go on strolling along St James's. 'When I have walked about a few times they will get used to it, and will take no notice.' These are stories of Cromwell in his days of glory, walking alone at night to gatecrash parties when he heard music, and nobody thought this in the least odd.

But now the man who appears on television is different from the rest of us. It does not matter any more what he does, he can just read the news aloud or predict the weather; what matters is that he appears nightly in a million sitting rooms. He can double his income by opening supermarkets, fame being the modern equivalent of the King's touch: by touching that supermarket door he has relieved it of its obscurity.

The writer Brian Darwent, having written the first biography of the novelist Jack Trevor Story, author of *The Trouble with Harry*, which Hitchcock filmed, had his manuscript returned by a publisher with this note: 'The problem in our opinion is that Jack Trevor Story is sadly not enough of a household name, and there are not enough famous people involved in the book to make it of sufficient interest to the general reader.' They liked the book, parts of which were hilarious, but that was no longer enough for 'the general reader', whoever he or she might be. The actual writing had nothing to do with it, as Jeffrey Archer, deciding to turn novelist, once told a friend who had protested that Archer couldn't write. He would, said that great man, *produce* a bestseller. And he did. When you are a celebrity there is little you can't do. When you are not, there is little that you can.

The serf out in the long fields of the Middle Ages, he had his place, as the poets of his time recognised. The man slumped in front of *EastEnders* has no place. If he opens a tabloid he will see its plot-lines reported as though these are real events, and he comes to believe they are of more importance than anything in his own life: in the process a man dwindles. 'When I get to Heaven, they will ask me what I did,' a lorry driver once said to me. 'And I shall say, "I was a *consumer*."' But for others there is the terrible underside of the celebrity cult, resulting in the stalker and the loon with the sniper's rifle, both intent on smashing their way into the goldfish bowl of fame.

When I started writing magazines and newspapers it was still, just, possible to write about people known only to their relatives and friends, even though nobody else seemed to. As Susannah Hickling, deputy editor of *Readers Digest* said, 'You always had this odd idea that ordinary people could be interesting.' In the following pages you will not meet anyone with a press agent or a publicist, or with a film or pop tour to promote. Only two of these people, the poet R.S. Thomas and the Duchess of Argyll, will be already known to you. The rest are tramps and villagers and squires: you will eat scones with a hangman in retirement, meet a pensioner whose one hobby is to sit A levels, and another who one evening, fishing for salmon, caught something the size of a basking shark; for some of them did do extraordinary things. Others, like the man who daily entertains his friends to tea, just went on being themselves; one fell off a church; one attended a television studio debate, but did not speak. Tush, man, as old Falstaff and many features editors have said, mortal men, mortal men. Yet for me, in the process most entered heroic myth.

If anything has underwritten this collection, it has been those lines by W.H. Auden,

> Private faces in public places
> Are wiser and nicer
> Than public faces in private places.

It has been a bizarre career. I doubt if anyone else would want to follow it, or could, any more.

BYRON ROGERS, 2001

Speak to the animals

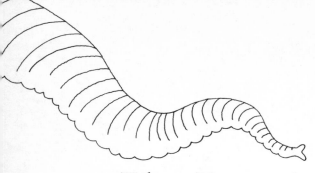

The Tortoise and
the Great War

T HE PASHA WAS in his seraglio; he was eating a lettuce.
From time to time the Pasha interrupted his lunch to
lurch irritably over to his three dozing concubines, all of
whom continued to sleep. He is thought to be 100 years old this
year though no one, least of all the Pasha himself, can be sure.

In the past month he has been visited by BBC Radio Wales,
reporters from the local and national press, Radio Orwell, UPI
International Broadcasting and a photographer from a German
colour magazine. The Pasha must be used to such attention by
now, for with every spring, newspapermen come to a house
outside Lowestoft to pick him up and scratch his head and take
photographs. They come to see Ali Pasha, the only Turkish
prisoner of war still in British hands. The Pasha is a tortoise.

On 6 May 1915 Henry Friston, a 21-year-old seaman, rejoined
his battleship, HMS *Implacable*, after ten days in Hell. Hell was just
200 yards long by 8 yards wide, and on British Naval maps was
known as X Beach in the Dardanelles, being too small even to
have a name. But in May 1915, men died there in their hundreds,

and the din — of British Naval bombardment and Turkish machine-guns — did not stop by day or night. Henry Friston, ferrying the wounded, had been under fire for ten days, had not eaten in three and not slept for two nights. But at this point military history stops and common sense falters, for Henry Friston was one of the world's great hoarders. Somehow, in the midst of all the bombardments on a crowded beach he picked up a tortoise, and, when he left Gallipoli, the tortoise went too, in his haversack.

'Before us lies an adventure unprecedented in modern war,' the commanding general, Sir Ian Hamilton, had declared in a force order a fortnight before. And for Ali Pasha, a Turkish tortoise, fully-grown at about at around 30 years old, the unprecedented adventure was just beginning.

He lived for a year in the gun-pit of a battleship on active service, sliding all over the place in rough weather, as Henry Friston recalled later. But how he managed to remain undetected is a complete mystery. The routine on board a battleship was strict, especially a battleship at war, and as Henry's son Don reflected, 'Tortoises make messes'. Then it was over, and Henry brought him home to Lowestoft; Ali Pasha was about to become a household god. 'He was always there,' said Don Friston, who works for a Lowestoft design group. 'He had been there 20 years before I was born.'

When Henry married in 1921 the tortoise passed to his mother; when she died in 1951 it came back to Henry again; after his death in 1977 it passed to Don. He has pictures of the tortoise with the generations, Henry ageing visibly in each one but Ali Pasha remaining exactly the same. Don Friston is now 47 and expects the tortoise to outlive him and become the pet of his grandchildren, as yet unborn. Some remote generation might just have the shell, he said, but as long as there were Fristons in Lowestoft there would also be an Ali Pasha.

This is not a story about pets, though the Pasha's fame has spread and for the last 20 years he has been the only non-canine honorary life member of the Tail-Waggers' Club of Australia, 70,000 strong. Nor is it about military history. It is about one man's ability, in the midst of the most extraordinary circumstances he would ever encounter, to go on being himself. In Gallipoli Henry Friston found a tortoise.

'Dad never threw anything away,' said Don Friston. He kept everything. When he left school in 1908 to become a gardener (the Fristons were fishermen or gardeners) he kept the certificate of attendance presented to him by his headmaster. When he signed on for the Royal Navy in 1912 he kept the oiled parchment ('Denomination: Free Methodist; Can Swim: Yes'). Even in the war he kept the bizarre little humorous monthly which the *Implacable*'s crew produced throughout its duration, which, more than any other thing, showed the overwhelming military superiority of the Royal Navy. One item, a spoof of a romantic novel, began: 'The gown showed off her exquisite figure to advantage. Her lovely face was lit up by a rosy blush and a radiance that is only obtainable by constant use of the very cheapest rouge...'.

Henry Friston kept maps and generals' memoirs and Turkish bullets and shrapnel and a Turkish army spoon. Ali Pasha never stood a chance. 'It must have been as common as us seeing rabbits,' said Don Friston, 'the only difference being that tortoises are easier to catch.'

His father, he said, was an odd sort of bloke. He had been very quiet, fond of gardening and fishing – fond of quiet, really. After he came back from the war he announced his intention of never going on his travels again and there were no family holidays; the only time Henry Friston left Lowestoft was to go to Llandudno for a week's Home Guard training. The only house he ever owned was a railway carriage.

'He'd bought this plot of land, intending to build on it, and he had this old railway carriage which he converted.' Don Friston unrolled a sheet of paper; his father had even kept his plans. 'But then the 1930s' slump came and then the war, and when that was over he was refused planning permission because they'd decided to extend the roads.'

Yet this very private man was, in his later years, hardly out of the local paper. There was a photograph of him when he retired as a bus inspector in 1959, and the headline explained it all: OWNER OF ALI PASHA RETIRES FROM THE BUSES. 'It began in the 1950s, I think. Dad has driven a certain route all his life and he'd got to know the reporters, and they'd found out about the tortoise. As far as they were concerned, whenever Ali came out of hibernation, it was the perfect spring story: "It's here, Ali Pasha is awake."'

A wider fame came in 1968 when the *News of the World* invited readers to write about unusual war souvenirs. Men had kept bayonets and old packs of cigarettes, but from Lowestoft came a letter from a man saying he had taken a tortoise prisoner.

The Australian papers picked it up because of the Anzac associations with Gallipoli. It did not take long for the Tail-Wagger-in-chief to write from Melbourne, enclosing a badge and certificate of honorary life membership, and marvelling 'that a soldier amidst all the horror of war thought to care for a creature as unlikely as a tortoise'. Letters poured in from all round the world. 'Dad used to spend a lot of time with the tortoise. He used to talk to it and tell it what a good old boy it was. After mother died he would spend hours picking dandelions and bindweed for it to eat. Ali Pasha has always been very fond of dandelions.

'Every winter he'd put it away ever so carefully, placing layers of sand in a box with hay on top so it could bury itself, and then insulating this with old newspapers and sacking. Then, of course, it would wake up and all the fuss would start again. My father used to find it very funny. As far as he was concerned, all that had happened was that once on a beach he picked up something he liked and brought it home. And there he was, getting older, and the tortoise getting more and more famous.'

From a pile of newspaper cuttings, Don Friston unearthed his father's obituary. The tortoise, he said wryly, had even managed to get into that.

An Audience with
An Elephant

IT IS A WINTER afternoon, and two men are walking slowly across Woolwich Common. They are not alone, and the two are clearly in some awe of the shape that walks between them. This is a Christmas story.

She is the most successful showbiz figure of her generation, and the most controversial. Opposition to her career led three years ago to her enforced retirement, but now, like General MacArthur, she has returned. Within the past month she has opened the Christmas season at Harrods, appeared in the Royal Variety Performance at the Palladium, and last Wednesday, on a wall in the Theatre Museum in Covent Garden, put, between the handprints of Sir John Gielgud and Dame Peggy Ashcroft, her own unmistakable mark. She is sixteen years old. And all this to her has been mere interruptions in the long days during which she must cram 300lbs of food into herself, for she is 8ft 6ins in height and weighs 2½ tons. She is Rani, the last elephant in Gerry Cottle's circus.

Requests for photographs come by the sack-load, yet there are still places in Britain where she cannot go, for the country she ambles through in her 40-week working year is as politically fragmented as mediaeval Germany. The further Left a council, the more strident is its opposition to performing animals, so when a change of regime occurs Rani returns to the recreation grounds and the commons. The most dramatic single index to local government change, she will be in Battersea Park this Christmas, for the Greater London Council has gone and Wandsworth now rules over the coloured lights. But to further confuse her sense of political geography, she has been there before, hired out to the GLC in the days of its pomp, so that Mr Ken Livingstone could pass like Haroun al-Raschid through Battersea.

For she is not just a circus performer: she is the first and only elephant to be licensed to appear in public under the 'Dangerous Wild Animals Act'. For £1,000, her daily rate, you can invite her to your wedding, once the appropriate environmental health officer has been contacted and has given his permission after sturdily invoking the Deity a few times. She has appeared at supermarkets, Indian restaurants, once wriggled her way into a village hall, was most recently in *Indiana Jones and the Temple of Doom*, and will be familiar to millions from her endorsement of videos, rice, Turkish delight and cornflakes in TV advertisements. She has, it is claimed, opened more things than the cast of *EastEnders*.

'Once a day, nails,' said her keeper, Robert Raven, a railwayman's son from Norfolk. 'I oil them, for they'd crack otherwise. Twice a week I grease around her eyes. I wash her, brush her down, wait on her hand and foot.' It is a seven-days-a-week job, from 7.30 in the morning, when she has her bran and maize, with hay, so she can make little sandwiches, to 10.30 at night. He scratched his head, incredulous that it should have come to this, when his ambition once had merely been to join a circus. ('You have these ideas, when you're a little boy.') An elephant's servant, muttered Mr Raven.

He has been in service for eight years, during which time he has managed to fit in a marriage. 'The wife's convinced she's jealous of her. We went for a walk once, the three of us, and I must have said something for the wife started hitting me and I shouted, "Help." The next thing we knew, the elephant was rushing towards us. I managed to stop her, but when you've seen an elephant running towards you it's a sight you don't forget in a hurry. I am very careful now.' Things are even further complicated by his baby son, who is fascinated by the animal, and whenever he manages to get out of their caravan crawls towards her tent; the elephant is nervous of small things.

The tent is a lean-to, with the flaps down to prevent the draughts to which an elephant is susceptible. Inside this she is chained, mainly on account of her curiosity. Water she associates with a black hosepipe, and with the number of black electric cables lying around the encampment a curious elephant wandering around would be a major hazard. 'Plus the fact that she's badly spoiled,' said Robert Raven. 'She was very ill once and went to stay with a vet, who let her do anything she wanted on his farm. She made a hole once in a barn wall just to see what was going on, and if she wanted to go into a field she'd just walk through a closed gate. He'd stand there smiling and smoking a cigar.'

The illness was in 1977, when her skin began flaking away, a condition that baffled the vets and was cured only when details were sent to Bombay University. It was suggested that the vegetables and fruit in her diet be increased. 'We were so worried, and then she recovered,' said Gerry Cottle. 'I suppose that made her special.'

Cottle bought her in 1973, a tiny elephant from north-west

India who turned up at Stansted with her mahout. He has good reason to remember it, for when he got there he was informed that VAT, which had been introduced a week earlier, applied to elephants. He lost £250,000 in the next two years because circus audiences appeared to agree with the councils that animals were a persecuted minority. When he went back into animals he had a vicar in to bless them and, to cock a snook at authority, added a turkey. The turkey, which does nothing except walk up and down, is called Lucky.

Twice a night, for seven minutes at a time, Rani steps from tub to tub, or walks over people. ('Being the only animal which can't jump, an elephant has to be sure-footed. She could walk on an egg.') She also plays cricket but has refused to play football. 'And what else would she be doing?' Robert Raven stroked one huge wrinkled side. 'Humping timber or walking up and down in a zoo.'

However often you have seen elephants, the bulk close up is bewildering. This, and the fact that the animal is never still, the body swaying from side to side, the whiskery trunk, in perpetual motion conveying food to the strange pink little mouth, prompting unease. I had brought a big bag of windfalls, which she ate one after the other, then did a quick professional frisk of my person. Apart from that she seemed to be engrossed in a private world.

'Oddly enough, I used to be frightened of dogs.' We had taken her for a walk. 'I suppose it's dangerous work, for more injuries are caused by an elephant than any other animal. Most of it's accidental, caused through sheer weight.' He stared at the great shape. 'When we go for a walk like this she hovers round me. She might chase a bit of paper but she never goes far. Does she like me? I don't know, she does as I tell her, but it's hard to say. Still, we have a good time — we go everywhere. We went into the sea once, only she went in a bit far.' In their time together he has managed to potty-train her, and a large black bin accompanies this curious pair on their social round. 'She'll go anywhere with me, and because of her I've been to places I wouldn't have been to, met people I'd never have met.'

He stopped, the elephant stopped and even the sinking sun seemed to stop. 'He's not a bad chap, that Harrison Ford,' said Robert Raven.

Wales

It Came as a
Big Surprise

T HERE IS AN Angler's Prayer you still come across occasionally, painted on old mugs in fishing inns. It is a bit like a river itself, the couplet meandering towards a tired rhyme.

> *Lord, grant that I may catch a fish so big that even I,*
> *When speaking of it afterwards, may have no need to lie.*

This is an account of a man, 'an excellent angler, and now with God', as Walton put it, who did just that. He caught a fish so big it would have needed two large men, their arms fully outstretched, to give cynics in saloon bars even a hint of its dimensions.

But he did more than that. He went fishing for salmon one day and caught something so peculiar, so far removed from even the footnotes of angling in Britain, that a grown man who was present ran off across the fields. Nobody would have thought it at all odd that day if the fisherman had been found trying to look up his catch in the Book of Revelations.

It needs a photograph. The fisherman is dead, his friends are beginning to die, and, had a photograph not been taken, few people would now believe what happened. A hundred years ago ballads and hearsay would have wrecked it on the wilder shores of myth; as it is, yellowing cuttings from the local paper, almost crumbling into carbon, are slowly unfolded from wallets, a print is unearthed reverently from under a pile of household receipts.

It was on 28 July 1933 that Alec Allen caught his fish, but even that has been elbowed into myth. His obituary (far from the national press) says that it was on 9 July. The *Guinness Book of Records* says that it was 25 July. But the one contemporary cutting had no doubts. It was 28 July. Appropriately, it was a Friday.

The photograph is extraordinary. Allen, a short man in a Fairisle pullover and baggy trousers, leans against a wall beside a trestle. It is a typical 1930s snapshot slouch. His hands are in his pockets, there is a cigarette in his mouth. But of course you notice all this a long time afterwards, because of the thing dangling from the trestle.

At first it looks like the biggest herring in the history of the sea. It towers over the man by a good 4 feet, a fish certainly, but the head ends in a dark snout, and the body appears to be armoured. The surroundings, a farm gate, the field beyond, underline the oddness, for in a farmyard a man is posing beside a thing the size of a basking shark. Alec Allen had caught himself a Royal Sturgeon in the River Towy, at Nantgaredig, near Carmarthen. It was 9 feet 2 inches long, had a girth of 59 inches and weighed 388 pounds.

Allen was a commercial traveller from Penarth in Glamorganshire, a well known sportsman and hockey referee who in later life was to referee Olympic matches. He was then in his early forties, one of that oddly innocent breed who figure in Saki and Wodehouse, but who latterly seem to have become as extinct as the Great Auk, the sporting bachelor. His great delight was fishing, but in him it was more than a delight. His great friend was Alderman David Price of Nantgaredig, who had known Allen all his life. All they had ever talked about, he recalled with wonder, was fishing.

In 1933 Allen was traveller for a firm of fishing tackle manufacturers. His father, also a great fisherman, was a traveller for a wallpaper firm, and father and son somehow contrived it that they could travel together in the same car. Both their commercial beats were West Wales, but theirs was a West Wales wonderfully concentrated between the rivers Wye, Teify and Towy. When their friends talk about the Allens it is with amusement, for it was notorious that their business rounds were designed for fishing.

Off-stage Hitler was ranting, Stalin drawing up lists of victims. Ramsay MacDonald droned his platitudes, and the dole queues lengthened. But in West Wales the Allens went their way, in a car full of tackle and wallpaper, their itineraries perfectly arranged to end in fishing inns beside rivers. The thing has an idyllic quality. It may have been a bit tough on you if your wallpaper shop was nowhere near a river, but nobody seems to have complained. In time the son succeeded the father as wallpaper salesman, but the itineraries did not change.

The two had rented a stretch of the Towy since 1928, which included some of the deepest pools in the river. But the summer of 1933 had been dry, the water level low, when, walking by one of the pools that July, Alec Allen noted enormous waves suddenly cross it. It puzzled him, but at the time he would have discounted any suspicion that they had been made by a living thing, for it was 15 miles to the sea, and tidal water ended 2 miles lower down.

A few days later Allen returned to the pool. It was evening, he had a friend with him, Edwin Lewis of Crosshands, and there was

a third man, his name lost to history, watching on the bank. Allen
began fishing, and at first it was a very quiet evening. But then he
felt a slight tug on his line. He pulled on it but this had no effect.

Alderman Price was fond of telling what happened next, 'Alec
used to tell me that he thought he'd hooked a log. He couldn't see
what it was, except that it was something huge in the shadows.
Then the log began to move upstream.' A faint smile would come
over Price's face. 'Now Alec knew that logs don't move upstream.'

Allen had still no idea of what was in the river. A more imaginative man might have become frightened at that stage, for his line
was jerking out under a momentum he had never experienced. In
the darkness of the pool he had hooked something which moved
with the force of a shark. He played it for 20 minutes, letting the
line move out when it went away, and, when it came back, retreat-
ing up the bank. But there was no channel of deep water leading
away from the pool; if there had been, no salmon line made
would have held his catch. Then he saw it.

Suddenly the creature leapt out of the water. Maddened, it
crashed into a shallow run, and there, under them threshing in the
low water, Allen was confronted by a bulk that was just not possible. The sightseer ran shouting for his life. Lewis ran forward with
the gaff, which he stuck it into the fish, but the fish moved and
this straightened the thing. Then the great tail flicked up and
caught Lewis, and threw him into the air on to the bank. Just one
flick, but it nearly broke the man's leg. There was a large rock on
the bank. Allen dropped the rod (it had been a freak catch, the
hook snagging in the fish's head, a sturgeon having no mouth) and
tugged at the rock. With it in his hands he waded out and
dropped it on the head, lifting it again and pounding at it. The
creature began to die, watched by two men who had no idea as to
what it was.

But in death it provided them with an even greater problem: how were they to get it out of the river? Allen ran to a nearby farm, and there occurred one of those rare moments that are pure comedy. Allen asked could he borrow a horse and cart, and the farmer, naturally, asked why. Allen said he had caught a fish. It ended with the farmer, farmer's friends, dogs, horse, cart and all going back to the bank.

'I can remember it now,' said Alderman Price. 'Alec came running to my house. I had never seen him so excited. All he would say was, "Well, I've caught something this time that you'll never beat." I went back with him. They'd pulled it up on to the trestle you see in the photographs, and the news had got round. People were coming in cars and in carts. They were ferrying children across the river.

'It had these big scales, I remember that. And it was very slimy. It was a sort of black and white in colour. No, I wasn't frightened.' He was in the habit of pausing at that point. 'It was dead.'

As the anglers gathered it was determined that the thing out of the river was a sturgeon. Vague memories stirred. Was it not the law that a landed sturgeon was the King's prerogative? A telegram was sent to Buckingham Palace inquiring after the King the next day, and a stiff little reply came the same day that the King was not in residence. Such trivia did not deter a man who had hooked the biggest river fish in recorded angling history. Allen sold the sturgeon to a fishmonger from Swansea for two pounds ten shillings, which worked out at something like a penny ha'penny a pound, this at a time when Scotch salmon at Billingsgate was fetching two and six a pound. More than 40 years later Allen's friends, who had helped him load the thing on to the train, were still bitter about the deal. There had been so much caviar in the sturgeon some of this had fallen on to the farmyard where it was eaten by the farmer's pigs. But selling it did get rid of one problem. There were no refrigerators in the valley, and 388 pounds of sturgeon was a lot of fish.

Allen fished on until his death in 1972 at the age of 77. In photographs the lean figure became stocky. Spectacles were added. Catches got held up regularly to the camera, something he could never have done that wild July night when he was content just to pose beside his fish. So had he considered the rest of his fishing life a sort of epilogue?

Brian Rudge, who ran the fishing tackle firm on whose behalf Allen meandered through West Wales, knew him well. 'I think he saw the incident as more of a joke than anything, he wasn't a man who was easily impressed. I think, you know, that as far as he was concerned it was a bit of a nuisance. He was out salmon fishing. The sturgeon had got in his way.' Alderman Price heard Allen talk about it a few times. 'It was usually when he heard anglers going on about their catches. He wasn't a boasting man but sometimes he couldn't resist saying, "Well, I suppose this would be the biggest fish I ever caught." And then of course they'd say, "Good God."'

Yet outside the valley and angling circles it was a small fame. There was no mention of it in the national press that July, and it was a small item even in the *Carmarthen Journal*. The august organ rose to its greatest heights of sensationalism. 'Two anglers had an exciting time while fishing in the River Towy,' the report began.

In March 1972 Allen died suddenly at the home in Penarth he had shared with a spinster sister, and there was a passage in his will which surprised his friends almost as much as the catching of the sturgeon. Though he had talked little about the incident, he left instructions that his body be cremated and the ashes put into the river at the spot out of which he had pulled Leviathan.

'I called on David Price one day,' said Ronald Jones, the former Chief Constable of Dyfed, and another of Allen's friends, 'and said what a pity it was about Alec. "Aye," said Dai, "I've got him there on the mantelpiece." It was the casket, you see. We were all surprised. Nobody had ever heard of anyone wanting that done before.'

'I suppose it was a romantic touch,' said Brian Rudge, 'but he wasn't the sort of man who'd like people to gather round a grave.'

It was a grey wet day when they put the ashes into the water. A dozen of his old friends, contacted by phone or letter, gathered on the bank, but no clergyman or minister had agreed to take part, their religion not recognising a river as consecrated ground. And, despite the hymns in the rain, it would seem to have had pagan overtones. Among the first things a people names are rivers. River gods are the oldest of all, so a man who had pulled out of a river its largest living thing would seem to be assuaging prehistory, having himself put back in its place.

'We said the Lord's Prayer,' said the Chief Constable, 'as we committed the ashes to the waters he'd fished for 50 years. But then as the wind carried them I saw a trout leap into the air just where they were drifting.

'And I said to Dai, "Look, Alec's there."'

The Lost Children

YOU WILL SEARCH in vain in any road atlas. I could not understand this when I started looking. I thought there had to be some small country town: the name breathed all the certainties of such a place. Sempringham. I could see the cobbled market square, the single Indian restaurant, the gleaming brass plaques on Georgian houses which bulged with solicitors. I knew it was in Lincolnshire but there was no sign of it on the map in that geometry of straight lanes and fens. What made it even more mysterious, and will puzzle those of you who read medieval history, is that this is such a familiar name; it is there in all the indices. Sempringham, where the lost children were...

It is 11 November 1283, and a king is writing to the Prior and Prioress of Sempringham. Edward I, the conqueror of Wales, has a request to make, 'having the Lord before our eyes, pitying also her sex and age, that the innocent may not seem to atone for the iniquity and ill-doing of the wicked and contemplating, especially, the life of your Order'. But you can forget the phrases, typical of that legalistic and self righteous man; the King was making the Prior and Prioress an offer they could not refuse. He wanted a child to disappear.

With a dangled pension of £20 a year there came an orphaned baby, the only child of the first and last Prince of Wales, Llywelyn, but to the King a biological time-bomb. She must never be allowed to marry or have children, and so Edward was ordering them to make her into a nun. When his troopers brought her father's few treasures out of his shattered principality, the coronet called the Crown of Arthur and the fragment of the True Cross, they brought her as well to Edward, in her cradle out of Snowdonia. She would never return.

Her name was Gwenllian, but the King's clerks got that wrong, spelling it Wencilian. She had 54 years of life left among strangers who would never learn to spell it, for it is Wencialian to the end in the Priory records. More poignantly she may never have learnt to spell it herself, or even to pronounce it, for in her one letter, an appeal for money (the letters of the Middle Ages were either about money or the law), it is Wentliane.

Her father Llywelyn was dead, killed in battle in December 1282, his severed head whitening on a pole above the Tower of London where it became a landmark (men could still see it fifteen years later from the pubs at the Tower's foot). With him had collapsed a Welsh nation state in its shaky beginnings, and a dynasty dating back to the Roman Empire which made the King's own family tree a thing of whimsy. But it is the private detail of the fall of the House of Gwynedd that is so overwhelming. Gwenllian's mother was dead, giving birth to her the previous June; her uncle's family had been hunted down. She was just seventeen months old when she was brought to the place of lost children.

You come on their names in footnotes for they are of little

interest to historians. They did nothing, they went nowhere; once those doors closed on them in childhood they were the dead. 'Three marks to be yearly laid aside to make good the wall and ditch to shut off the nuns, that no person may go in or have the least sight of them. No presents or messages to be delivered to or from the nuns. The windows through which anything is delivered to have wheels that turn so the sisters may not see anyone, or anyone see the sisters.' The rules at Sempringham of England's one monastic order, founded by the little hunchback Gilbert, were strict.

The children had committed one crime, that of being born. Even Stalin didn't hold that against the children of his victims, for eventually these were allowed to emerge from their orphanages. But not Gwenllian or her little girl cousins who turned up the following year before being dispersed to other nunneries; had they stayed together they might have shared some memory of the past, and to the English this was Year Zero. The little boys of Gwynedd did not come, they had disappeared into perpetual imprisonment. The children of disgraced English barons came, one or two to be retrieved when a deal was struck in later years. But the Welsh children were already history and for them Sempringham was the dustbin of a broken dynasty. But where *is* Sempringham?

Find Grantham on the map. Forget the alderman and his grocer's shop: follow the A52 eastwards until after about 9 miles you see a B road turning south to Billingborough and Bourne. Two miles after Billingborough you will find Sempringham, a place where Mrs Thatcher has probably never been.

Sempringham is a locked church at the end of an earth track, out in the fields with no houses near it. You will have no problem finding the church, for you will already have seen it from miles around; there is no landscape here, only sky. But once there was

something which would have pushed up that sky. What survives is
a church which was there when Gilbert came, but 350 yards to the
south of this he built his Priory, the nave of which was 55 feet
longer than Ripon Cathedral and 25 feet wider than Lichfield.
When archaeologists excavated here before the last war it was this
width which stunned them and the enormous buttresses which
flanked it; together they suggested a towering loftiness which
would have been one of the wonders of the Middle Ages.
The local newspaper was suitably impressed: 'Excavations at
Sempringham. Remains of a big church discovered.'

Of this there is now no trace for at the Dissolution it became a
quarry, the bumps still visible in the field being those of the mansion built from of its stones. Daniel Defoe saw that mansion
when he came through, and the tactful old hack recorded its plaster-
work was the equivalent of that in the Royal Palace of Nonesuch.
There is no trace of any of the graves, so hers is as lost as those of
the rest of her dynasty (though her great grandfather's stone
coffin lies empty in Llanrwst church); the English saw to it that
there were to be no shrines, and two generations on were hiring an
assassin in France to kill the last male member of the family. They
had forgotten about him.

She would have seen the church, though not in its present
form. It looks a bit odd now, having been restored from near ruin
by a Victorian parson; its huge original arches and the fussy little
chancel he added make it seem as though a giant's clothing had
been cut down to fit ordinary men.

There were 200 nuns in her time. A high wall ran the length of
the Priory and separated them from the 80 monks, so that there
were two altars, one on each side. Think of her there in those 54
years of institutional life. The coarse woollen clothing. The bells
ringing for worship and work, matins and masses, masses and

matins; the enforced silences which may have got easier as childhood ebbed; the windows squeaking as they turned on their
wheels for a few inches when a stranger called. She had come from
the mountains and she was to pass her life without seeing a single
hill. The wind howling over the flat land, and time passing.

Perhaps she grew cynical, watching the arrival of other bits of
jetsam, the children of her father's enemies. Roger Mortimer's
daughter came after he escaped from the Tower, a member of the
family suspected of the treachery which had led to her father's
death. The dustbin offered excellent views of English political
fortunes. The two daughters of the executed Hugh de Despencer
came, on a pension of £20 a year between them as they were not
such big potatoes. She, Gwenllian, was a very big potato. They
would not have allowed her to forget that. When Edward II tried
to raise cash from the Pope for Sempringham it was Gwenllian's
presence there that he mentioned. When Edward III came through
in 1327, the Priory records show that he confirmed her £20 a year,
but then the English could afford to be generous.

They had always had this small, nagging guilt when it came to
the Welsh, the Archbishop of Canterbury observing in 1199 that
'the Welsh, being sprung by unbroken succession from the original stock of Britons, boast of all Britain as theirs by right'. Which
was why, when her father's head was paraded down Cheapside, the
Londoners crowned it mockingly with ivy.

And now all that was over. Llywelyn's halls had been destroyed,
their timbers taken away, his archives burned, all this so
completely men now argue as to where his power had its seat, even
as to the form this took. There is one extraordinary little footnote: some years ago a family moved into a smallholding at Aber,
near Conway, and found under a Victorian grate a massive
medieval fireplace. Under the render of the walls they found mul-

lioned windows and the outline of a great arch; and Mrs Kathryn
Gibson who had bought a chicken farm found herself in the lost
hall of the princes, where Gwenllian had been born.

Perhaps she was happy in her long exile in Sempringham. I like
to think so, for everything else would be so sad; perhaps in time
there was a stout, bossy woman as masterful as her father had
been. The nuns would have been in awe of her anyway, let us hope
she exploited this to the hilt.

We can imagine this because, with one exception, none of the
lost children speak to us. The exception is her cousin Owain, who,
with his brother Llywelyn, had been sentenced to perpetual
imprisonment in Bristol castle. Llywelyn died after a few years but
Owain lived on, and 20 years later old King Edward was still wor-
rying about him. This, you may remember, was the king who in
public said that sin was not passed on. 'As the King wills that
Owain son of Dafydd ap Gruffydd who is in the Constable's cus-
tody in the castle, should be kept in future more securely, he
orders the Constable to cause a strong house within the castle to
be repaired as soon as possible, and to make a wooden cage bound
with iron in that house, in which Owain may be enclosed at night.'
Just like a mouse. That was in 1305.

But then something odd happened. Around 1312 Owain managed to get a letter out to the new king, Edward II, and his Council.
The one voice for the lost children in speaking. 'Owain, son of
Dafydd ap Gruffydd, shows that whereas he is by order of the
King detained in the Castle of Bristol in strong and close prison,
and has been since he was seven years old, for his father's trespass.
He prays the King that he may go and play within the wall of
the castle if he cannot have better grace of the King...'. It
sounds like the plea of a small boy, but it isn't. The man begging
to be allowed to play within the wall of the castle is 36 years

old; he has been locked up, probably without exercise, for 29 of them.

The Council ignored his appeal but was so startled to receive this, a hand has written across it in Latin, 'Let it be enquired who sues this petition.' They had forgotten who he was. What was this thing that had dared crawl into their daylight, this ghost out of history? It is like that scene in Koestler's *Darkness At Noon* when the purged Communist learns that the man in the next cell is a Tsarist, still alive. Owain was still alive in 1320, when a bureaucratic hand records a change of constable. Thereafter... nothing.

'1337. Wencilian, daughter of the Prince of Wales, died, after 54 years of life in the Order. The King excuses the Prior and the convent from a payment of £39.15s.4d...'. That payment was tax they were owing, but the King was grateful; a child had disappeared.

I walked up the track through the fields and, seeing something in the grass, bent down. It was a dead barn owl, the first I had seen, and, ruffling in the beautiful orange plumage to find a cause of death, I came on a tiny metal ring crowded with writing around one leg. It gave instructions so I wrote to the British Museum of Natural History, saying where and when I had found it. A month later a reply came. The bird had been hand-reared and had lived just 96 days, travelling only a mile and a quarter from its place of release. Its natural habitats had gone, there were so few barns now. But I kept the ring. At Sempringham I had found another small thing lost in a huge world.

The Last Tramp

B Y THE TIME YOU read this the subject of the article will have disappeared into Wales as effectively as any goblin or guerilla of the Middle Ages, as completely, in fact, as David Livingstone disappeared into Africa. George Gibbs is one of that shrinking body of men steadily eroded by the processes of government who can still do this, as for nine months of every year, in 20th-century Britain, he is beyond the reach of postmen and phone calls. Gibbs comes at the end of a very long tradition: at 53 he is the last of the wanderers.

For as long as there have been hearth fires and home acres some men have been forsaking them, to wander. Outraged legislation indexed their progress, spitting against 'vagabondes, roges, masterless men and idle persons' and 'myghty vagabonds and beggars'; up until the nineteenth century, with its glimmerings of official enlightenment, society hounded and reviled its tramps because in their way they represented, like Soviet emigrants, an adverse comment upon it. Yet then tramps acquired a haze of romance, particularly with growing urbanisation. They were the men outside, the bronzed wanderers, men with no axes to grind (though ironically this is how many earned their livings), with no families, no past, no future. The romance was, of course, in contradiction of the facts. Tramps, the manager of a reception centre told me, were usually 'physically or mentally disabled, or socially inadequate'. Besides, very few of them now did wander: what remained were derelicts or alcoholics shuffling through city centres. Philip O'Connor, author of *Vagrancy*, advised me to invent such a man: he doubted whether he existed in life.

Finally, I found George Gibbs. Since 1968 he has been something of a minor celebrity in Wales. Then, trying to light a fire in a deserted house near Llanelly, he had the good fortune first to push his hand up the chimney, and enough blasting powder came tumbling down to have sent him, the house, and most of the street, into kingdom come. It was the year before the Investiture.

Gibbs spent his winters at the Stormydown Reception Centre near Bridgend, leaving each year with the spring, and by summer could be anywhere between Glamorgan and Anglesey; the difficulties in contacting a tramp are legion. I rang some of his regular stops — a Carmarthenshire farmhouse, a Newtown presbytery — without luck. But there was one thing which characterised Gibbs: his fondness for the police force. Like an unofficial Inspector of Constabulary, he dropped in on their stations, chatted to them, discussed their families, promotions, moves, smoked their cigarettes and drank their tea. The Dyfed-Powys force offered to pass the message 'up the line' as they put it, to say I was interested in meeting George. A week later I was rung up from Machynlleth: 'Mr Gibbs,' said a voice, 'is just entering town.' Which made him sound like a gunfighter.

It is 9.30 a.m. in Machynlleth. A smell of fresh bread drifts through the town. In the sky the first of the day's Royal Air Force jets are beginning their passes along the valley, as in the municipal rubbish tip George Gibbs is waking up. He has spent the night in an open shed which contains agricultural machinery, where across the entrance he has placed a series of planks and oil cans to deter intruders, so it is difficult at first to make him out in the gloom. Then there is a slight movement among a heap of old coats and sacking in the corner of the shed, and two large white eyes, like a lemur's, peer out. Somewhere in the huddle a radio is switched on and pop music flares in the darkness. Mr Gibbs is awake.

All night he has slept on some planking, covered by his coats, his feet in an old dog-food sack. He has slept well, as he always does. 'I can't sleep in a bedroom any more. I roll around all night. But when I sleep on a hard surface I sleep all night.' Gibbs has slept well in abandoned boats, in telephone boxes with his knees pulled up like a Mexican, even, he confesses shamefacedly, in public lavatories. But mostly he sleeps in far more comfortable surroundings, in empty houses, on dried bracken in snug barns. He walks some 8 miles a day. All over Wales he has places to sleep in at 8-mile intervals. After a week with him one begins to suspect that he has hides at such intervals to heaven.

It takes Gibbs a long time to get up. Finally, at 10.00 a.m., a small crumpled figure comes blinking into the morning. He is wearing an old black beret found on a rubbish tip, to which he has fixed a Women's Institute of Wales badge found on the roadside, a cavalry twill sports coat given to him by a Caernarvon lady, and a sweater issued at the reception centre. On his feet he has a pair of ladies' slippers found on Barmouth rubbish tip, which will be replaced that week by a pair of wellingtons found on Machynlleth rubbish tip. Rubbish tips to Gibbs are the equivalents of all those marvellous wrecks bursting with consumer goods in *Robinson Crusoe* and *Swiss Family Robinson*. He scours them, poking about in the packing cases and ashes, the seagulls' one rival. They clatter irritably up as he passes.

Gibbs is a curious, shuffling, knock-kneed little figure. He weighs very little, like most tramps – just 8 stone. Of a tramp found dead by the police, he told me: 'The sergeant who found him said he was just like a sheet of cardboard to lift, a sheet of cardboard. He'd been dead a fortnight, I think. Poor old Paddy.' He is bespectacled and bearded, and quite spectacularly grimy, a small boy's dream figure of personal hygiene. He talks occasionally of romantic little morning dips in the River Conway but cannot quite remember when he last had one. 'I prefer showers meself. It's clean water. In a bath you're lying in dirty water,' says George with the cold objectivity of a man who has not been in either for a very long time.

He was born in Glasgow in 1917, the son of a sailor missing at sea during World War I; he himself went straight to sea after leaving school, ending up as a cook, and took to the roads after his own wartime experiences as a merchant seaman. He left the sea, having had what amounted to a nervous breakdown, 'always thinking of the other ships that went up, the bombings and suchlike'. He told his mother he was off to look for work, and did work for a while as an itinerant agricultural labourer, but in 1948 he came to Wales and really went on the roads. He never told his mother he was a tramp: to the end of her life she believed he was a farmworker. The Gibbs family are not given to writing letters, and George does not know where his three sisters and brother are. Since 1948 he has been out of Wales twice, once when he went on a long tramp to Kent in the early 1950s, and contracted pneumonia, and once two years ago when he was given a rail warrant by the Stormydown Reception Centre to go home. On that occasion he found that his mother had died a few months earlier.

George is not very forthcoming as to the point when his itinerant

labouring tipped over into tramping, but it seems to have been a
quite gradual process. At first he worked regularly: now the last
time he remembers working was over six years ago, for five weeks
in a Flintshire brickworks. 'Quite interesting work,' he says airily.
On tramping itself he says, 'Once you get on to the road it gets
into the system. It's like smoking: you get a craving. I just can't get
off.'

At Machynlleth he has just lit his fire and is perched in front of
it like a small Fisher King, dangling his billy can in the flames at
the end of a stick. George puts his tea in the bottom of the can
and allows the water to boil up through it so one can almost eat
the resulting mixture with a knife and fork. As he sits he talks in a
soft, unflurried monotone no incident can disturb. George says
'Oh dear' a lot of the time; as an exclamation it covers the gamut
of his feelings, which seem to run from mild surprise to mild
upset. When we found a huge black catamaran beached miles
from anywhere on a remote beach near Aberdovey: 'What have we
here? Dear, o dear,' he repeated in surprise. Again, when he saw
some modernised buildings, 'Ruined that, they 'ave... dear, o
dear.' George is like a whitewashed wall: one longs to scribble all
over it, to make some kind of impression.

He is proud of being on the roads. On page after page of the
occasional notebooks he keeps are reflections on the life and the
lore. He lists the old tramping signs that were once scored on
trees: does he ever make them himself? 'No, I never do. Who's to
read them?' The signs fall into two categories, invitations and
warnings; the latter seem to be more numerous. Thus a circle
bisected means that the householder could call the police Ø; Z
indicates extreme warning, the tramp should move on at once.
Others are amusing: two axe-like symbols mean that the house-

holder will help the tramp, but will also expect work first; a triangle means the house is a police house. A circle is the symbol of a generous person, two small concentric circles of a rich person. Poring over this lore, George communicates it to nobody.

He did, however, earlier this year meet an Irishman travelling south. 'He only had a little bag, no frying-up equipment...'. A long pause. 'I think he was a hitch-hiker.' This is George's most telling recrimination against a fellow wanderer.

He himself is anxious to establish his credentials. 'I think I must be the only fellow on the road with a radio.' 'I think I've got the only pram with two reflectors on it.' 'I think I must be the only man on the road who's had six prams.' On the sides of his pram he has written the names of the Welsh towns through which he passes. He was given it by a café owner in Caernarvonshire: the pram is battered and old, but to George it is wardrobe, medicine cupboard, desk, larder and trunk.

Today, as he begins to pack up after the night, it contains a ground sheet (a piece of wartime barrage balloon found years before on some forgotten rubbish tip), two radios (both of them gifts), a first aid box, an old cap with ear muffs, two very clean towels and a shaving kit (says heavily-bearded George of the latter, 'It's in case I go anywhere special'), mending threads and needles, a pair of sunglasses, the Bible, a camera (a gift for which he cannot afford films), a toilet roll, a knife, fork and spoon, some lard (which he prefers, as more nourishing, to butter), tea, sugar, an elderly pork pie, some cereals, a bottle of VP wine (his one alcoholic drink), a bottle of paraffin for his spirit lamp, a wrapped up frying pan, some lighter fuel for his stick lighter (another gift) and a pair of shoes too large for him to wear but too new to throw away. 'I've got everything,' reflects George, 'except the kitchen sink.'

The pram also contains his occasional books, old notebooks he has found or been given. On one, in a large, round, child-like hand he has written 'George Gibbs Esq., Scotstoun, Glasgow, Scotland': it was the last time he had an address, a quarter of a century ago. He records in these books, in a weird macaronic mixture of Welsh and English, the deaths of his heroes: 'Judy Garland found dead in her flat, Chelsea, Mehefin 22, 1969. Dydd Sul.' In another I came upon the fruit of 25 years' tramping, a neat list of Welsh convents, presbyteries and colleges with crosses, and circles to mark the degree of their hospitality. There is also a list of the best places to sleep (it includes a police cell).

Strangest of all there is a roster of police names: force after force, town after village, the constables, sergeants, inspectors. George notes their progress with the attention of a herald to a ruling caste, and supplements these with cuttings from local papers so the plump, untroubled faces beam out at one. Some have signed their own names. The police force has no more uncritical lay admirer than George Gibbs.

His passions, in fact, are two: the police and Wales. There are Welsh-English word lists, sad little dates from Welsh history, even this touching entry: 'Give me the Welsh-speaking people any day. They are more kindly and friendly. I will stay in Cymru, and be buried here.' The Welsh, he says, are sympathetic to tramps. 'But don't put that down,' he says in sudden unfeigned alarm. 'You'll have the English coming over.' He has taken all Wales to be his bedroom.

From Machynlleth George was turning south. In the three months since he had left Stormydown he had moved north in a slow arc towards Anglesey and was now going south along the coast. He travels his 8 miles on a good day, but intersperses these with rest days at intervals. 'It's not an easy life. I wouldn't advise anyone to take to the road. It was really tough when I used to roam in the winter, maybe two to three inches of snow. I have difficulty getting my old pram through snow.'

He is fortunate in having good health. Apart from his pneumonia in the early 1950s he has been ill only once, when he went down with flu at Christmas time, 1969, having been soaked in a downpour on the way to Stormydown. The flu resulted in a spot on his lungs and he had to spend a month in hospital. He says of himself: 'I've never been ill actually on the roads. Getting the air, day by day, and walking… quite healthy, me.' Yet he has little energy and tires easily. His teeth are bad. In his pram he has a jar of home-made jam which he has not opened in two years. 'Can't. It would play holy mackerel with my teeth, that.'

There is an even tenor to his life, which all untoward events disturb, to send great ripples across it. Thus I came across the news of my coming on different pages of his books. Yet he accepted me the way he accepts everything, and was soon introducing me to policemen. 'This is Mr Rogers. He is writing the history of my life.' They looked incredulously at his Boswell as we shuffled by.

George plans his trips in a very loose way. He has a vague overall target, like Anglesey, but changes his route as it pleases him. 'A man like myself going on steadily, not bothering anyone, bound for anywhere. Anywhere does me. A man who goes everywhere, bound for anywhere.' This is the week up to his stay in Machynlleth.

Tuesday night: A chicken shed, between Barmouth and Dolgellau. George has slept here before. The farmer, who has been here 20 years, says that, of all the tramps who once called, George is now the last. 'We would think now that there was something missing from the year if he didn't call.' George sleeps just outside the chicken wire. Piled neatly are some old paperbacks he left the year before, and which the farmer has let lie. Before he sleeps, George, who is unable to light a fire here, asks the farmer for some hot water for his tea. The chickens grieve and scuttle. 'Nice listening to the chickens,' says George, 'nicer than traffic.'

Wednesday: Towards Dolgellau. First stop Barmouth rubbish tip, where George spends an intent half hour, disturbing the seagulls and finding only some week-old newspapers. He collects the week-old papers. As night comes on he settles down for the night in an open barn some 2 miles from Dolgellau: he has walked some 7 miles. He lights a fire, drinks yet more tea.

Thursday: Towards Dolgellau. First stop Dr Williams' School, a girls' boarding school on the outskirts of Dolgellau. He always stops here. This time he knocks on the kitchen door and is given some roast beef sandwiches and tea. It is his first meal of the day. George reaches Dolgellau about midday and claims his Social Security benefit. This is the first breath of economics in his world. A tramp can claim a day's requirement, the amount of which is left to the local office, but which in George's case varies from 40p to 60p. At Dolgellau it is 60p. It is, in some ways, a cruel sum: just the minimum to keep a man alive. Yet to George it is a bonanza. Though he is entitled to the rate daily, the nature of his wanderings means that he rarely claims it more than twice a week. He encounters little difficulty at the Social Security offices as he is by now well-known to the officers. They fill in his name and age and seek to establish when he last claimed. Cases have occurred where the quick and the very quick among tramps have succeeded in getting to more than one office in a day, leaving a trail of benefit claims. With his 60p he buys milk, ten cigarettes, a packet of tea, and two pork pies. He begins the slow winding climb out of Dolgellau. The night is coming on as he wheels his pram over the pass towards Abergynolwyn, a slow little figure lost in an eternity of cloud and rock. He plays his radio. That night be sleeps in a barn under Cader Idris. It is his most romantic place, a foot deep in dried bracken. He lights his paraffin lamp, makes tea with hot water from a nearby guest house, and eats his two pork pies. And so to bed.

Friday: To Abergynolwyn. He rises at 10.00 a.m., his usual time, drinks some more tea, again with hot water from the guesthouse, and starts. It is a glorious day. He wheels his pram along the perimeter of Tal-y-llyn lake to the village, where he buys a tin of rice and calls on the policeman. He and PC Edwards talk about the old, dead tramps. 'They're a dying race,' says the policeman. His wife gives George some sandwiches and a pair of good old shoes. The shoes disappear into the pram. Everyone seems to be glad to see George. 'Oh, it's you,' says one old man. 'Now I know summer is really here. You're the first swallow.' George goes off the roads early, about 4.00 in the afternoon, as he is tired. Because of traffic, he is careful not to walk at night. He sleeps in an isolated little shed some miles from the village. As the dark comes in across the mountains, he lights a small fire, heats his rice and eats his sandwiches. He plays his radio into the small hours.

Saturday: To Towyn and beyond. On the way he passes one of his old sleeping places, or rather what remains of it. The place, an old cottage, has been demolished by the local council to make a lay-by. George mourns briefly for it: 'There was an old mattress there. I used to sweep the floor with my little brush.' At Ysguboriau Farm nearby, Mrs Gwenda Jones greets George: 'This was one of the old tramps' calls. We gave them bread and butter and tea. But they've all gone. This one must be the last of them.' We plod thoughtfully on, through Towyn, to a railway crossing house. But the night has come and is full of cars. George decides to stop at a

rubbish tip a mile from the house. Using the pram he drapes his
ground-sheet into a lean-to tent, lights a fire and fries some old
bacon, 'what you would call a rough lay-down'. The night is warm.

Sunday: A rest day. George ambles the last mile to the crossing
house. It is being modernised but the doors are still open. George
does not like the modernisation. 'Oh dear, all this was wooden
once, wooden floors, wooden walls here. They've ruined it. I was
quite warm. They've ruined it completely.' He eats little today,
some old bread and lard he has, and brews up. He plays his radio
endlessly, pop, political reports and drama wafting into the bowed
little head.

Monday: Towards Machynlleth. He walks 6 miles, calling at two
houses for some hot water where he is given some bread and a
couple of raw onions. He stops the night at a cluster of modernised little cottages standing in a courtyard, all for some reason
deserted. He makes a fire in the fireplace, fries his bread, and eats
it with raw onions. So far in the week he has only once asked permission of a farmer to stay the night: nobody minds, says George,
as long as he leaves the place tidy. Each morning he cleans up his
rubbish.

Tuesday: The last four miles to Machynlleth. He arrives early in
the afternoon, having called in the morning on the Rector of
Pennal, who gives him bread and butter, a cake and some tea, and
tells me that he too doesn't know what's become of the tramps. At
Machynlleth George goes to the Social Security office, and is
given 40p.

'I don't feel envious at seeing a family through a window in
winter. I hope they're not the same as I am. I wouldn't like anyone
else to be out in the weather like me. I see how happy they are at
their fire. It makes me happy. I had an experience once, about ten
years ago, in an old mansion near Oswestry. It hadn't been lived in

for ten to twelve years. I got up to the attic. I'd just set out my candles, an old newspaper to read, when I suddenly saw the paper rise to the height of one foot, or thereabouts. When I saw that I went all cold and shivery, the coldest I ever was. There was no draught. I packed up as quick as possible and got out. There was something in that room, I went down the stairs into the pitch-black. But I think I would stay there now. I've slept in graveyards, in the coke holes of cemeteries, nobody bothers you there. Kids don't come into graveyards, and the dead don't do any harm. It's the living you've got to watch.

'The old-timers are all dead now, either found dead on the roadside or in derelict buildings. I'm not worried about whether I'll be found dead. Everyone has to die, wherever he is, at sea, in a car, in a field, on a quayside. My ambition is to die in Wales, and be buried here.'

Like a swallow, he begins to move South. The holiday cars flooding into Machynlleth shy away from the intent little figure on the road, like horses shying from some creature which has somehow sidestepped the processes of evolution. He disappears into Wales.

Note: Mr Gibbs has now come in from the roads. Latterly he had taken to spending his winters in a hut at Lampeter Station, so the district council, seeking to raze the station, was obliged to offer him a home under the 1977 Homelessness Act. He was by then of pensionable age, and the council's action had made homeless a man for whom homelessness was a way of life. It has to be the most wonderful of all bureaucratic ironies. Mr Gibbs has exchanged his pram for a bungalow in Lampeter, and the last time we met he gave me a visiting card.

The Lost Lands

B Y EARLY AFTERNOON it was clear we were in a frontier zone. The country lanes had gone. These roads were wide, the tarmac well maintained, and there was military traffic now, jeeps and trucks, the drivers of which did not slow down as they passed. And then there was some kind of crossing point, unmanned but with a red flag flying over it. I braked to read a large notice in the two languages. 'Do Not Touch Any Military Debris. It May Explode And Kill You', which seemed reasonable enough. I pointed to the red flag.

'Oh, that's all right,' said the Farmer. 'They put those up to deter tourists. You'll be all right on this road.'

And so it was, at just after 2.00 p.m., with a cold wind blowing the rain so the horizons kept coming and going, that we passed into the Lost Lands.

Just after the village of Trecastle, the A40, moving west from Brecon to Llandovery, enters a valley where the old coaching road has been straightened. On the skyline to the south is an even older road under grass and mud, along which Roman legionaries and medieval English kings passed. On the other side of the valley a lane runs up past Llywel church, and on to a part of Wales where in the 40 years I have used the A40 I have never dared go. Beyond that skyline lie the Lost Lands.

Epynt... You will not find it on any road sign, for this is an area which has disappeared from everything except the memories of the old and the schedules of the British Army, whose maps of a rectangle 12 miles by 15, not that much smaller than the Isle of Wight, are detailed. It was here that 60 years ago the Army compelled 219 men, women and children to leave 54 farms and smallholdings to make way for an artillery range. The Army is still there.

A truck went by, faces under red berets looking incuriously down at the car parked beside the road. 'Paras,' said the Farmer.

As they had driven along, the Farmer had been intoning a litany of names, the farms he remembered from when, as a young man, he had himself been forced to leave. Hirllwyn... the Long Tree. Gwybedog... the Place of the Gnats. Cefnioli... the Farmer stumbled over the translation of that one, for these were names old in his father's time and in his father's before him. One of those evicted claimed his family had been farming the Epynt when, had they existed, newspaper headlines would have been about the Wars of the Roses.

The Farmer was remembering people now. 'The old gentleman at Cwmioli, John Owen, the Army still let him graze his sheep on Epynt but each time he went back, a hedge would be down, a wall gone. He died of a broken heart. He said, "It was an end for me when Cwmioli went."' Thomas Morgan, Glandwr. 'He was so convinced he would return one day that he used to sneak back at night to light a fire in the old farmhouse. The Army must have seen the smoke, for in the end they blew the house up.

Mind you, I don't know why he bothered, he and his brother had been too frightened to sleep there for years because it was haunted.'

'What happened to the ghost?'

'Oh, the Army blew that up as well.'

Sometimes the farms were a heap of stones among the trees, sometimes not even a bump in the ground showed that generations had lived there. Occasionally, and this was bizarre, the Army had rebuilt the farmhouse to provide bivouacs for their men, so these stood blank and empty, but far more immaculate than they had been in life.

The Army had also built shell houses to train their troopers to react to the snipers of Northern Ireland, and a folly of eighteenth-century proportions, an entire high-roofed East German village in which to rehearse street warfare against the Warsaw Pact. They went into such detail on this (adding a cemetery and, to the indignation of the devout, a church), they had only just completed it, at God (and the MOD) knows what cost, when the Berlin Wall came down and the Warsaw Pact disappeared like snow in water. An East German village stands forlorn on a Welsh mountain, part of it used as a rubbish tip.

Under some pines, ringed by a huge sky, is the old Drovers Arms, at a crossroads where the paths of prehistory meet. 'This inn was once a welcome resting place on the old drovers' routes. . . . Renovated 1994.' I could see the green tracks winding away up the mountain, but a pole had been lowered and there was another sign, not reasonable this time, but peremptory. 'Danger. Keep Out.' And more red flags.

'There's a view for you,' said the Farmer. From where we stood we could see hills, and hills behind the hills, and mountains beyond these. Then... Ker-POW. A huge dull noise, as though a man 7 miles high, suffering from a smoker's cough, had cleared his throat above the clouds.

'Is that thunder?' asked the Farmer. Ker-POW. 'No,' he answered himself. 'Time to be off, I think.'

There had been some talk of visiting the East German village and the Farmer had thought this might be possible, for the cold war, he said with irrefutable logic, was over. The two of us stared at its red roofs below us, but at that moment a star-shell burst lazily over it. 'Though not today,' said the Farmer.

We passed a little graveyard and the perfectly repointed bits of wall, which were all that remained of a chapel. Here, private subscription has raised a plaque on which there is a translation from the Welsh.

> I remember the prayer meetings
> And the children's Sunday School,
> And how many had walked
> Over the hills and dales.
> I will remember them as long as I live.
>   Amie Williams, 1996

We had reached a high point, where we stopped and walked, bent against the wind. 'My old home is down there,' said the Farmer suddenly. 'Just beyond East Germany.'

He is in his 80s now, a merry, mischievous man, who in his long life has been farmer, milkman, caretaker, horse dealer and proprietor of a chip shop and, having flown over all these, still competes in sheepdog trials though he owns no sheep. 'I find myself thinking more and more about this place now, and of what might have been.'

And I thought of the passage quoted by the historian, Herbert Hughes, in his *An Uprooted Community*, in which Iorwerth Peate, founder of the Welsh Folk Museum, records his meeting with an old lady. She was 82, and, as the two watched her furniture being loaded on to a lorry, she asked Peate where he was from, a question the Welsh always ask. He said he was from Cardiff. 'My dear boy,' she said, 'go back there as soon as you can, it is the end of the world here.'

It was a time of national emergency. 'They told us it was either them or the Germans,' said Iorwerth Davies, late of Gwybedog. But there was still a great sense of injustice. At the time the Army had requisitioned 56,000 acres of England, 6,000 acres of Scotland, but they had taken 70,000 acres of Wales, so a country one-tenth the size of the other two had more land taken away than both of them together.

And there was something else. 'In the London ministries they thought they were dealing with a largely unpopulated area on the Epynt,' said Herbert Hughes. 'But they weren't.' What they were dealing with was something they and their colleagues had never encountered, a Welsh community that had changed little since the Middle Ages. Many spoke no English. The former MP, Gwynfor Evans, remembers a court case involving some minor breach of wartime agricultural regulations in which two of the evicted Epynt farmers were forced to pay for the services of a translator. 'I had been in courts where Arabs and Spaniards had appeared and had translators provided for them. But these men, speaking their own language in their native land, had to pay. The outcry eventually led to the Welsh Courts Act.'

It was a pastoral, self-sufficient society that medieval travellers would have recognised. There were no villages, no roads, and travel was on horseback, the women riding side-saddle. 'My uncle used to come and visit us only in the summer, but only if it was a dry summer,' said Iorwerth Davies. 'I remember my mother taking us to market in a horse and trap, and, when it came to rain, pulling a leather blanket over us. I looked out and saw the moon, but when we came round a hill the moon was on the other side of us. "Mam, mam, the moon's moved." The only cars we saw belonged to the district nurse and the school inspector. If a plane came over, we were allowed out of school to watch.'

The only travel was with the flocks or to market. Every visit to a town was an opportunity to take on supplies, however small, before the wet autumns came, and with them a stock-taking of coal, flour, yeast, sugar and salt to see whether there was enough to get through the winter. One farmer, caught in a snowstorm with his wife while returning from market, reassured her. 'Look at it this way, once we're home we'll be all right 'til Easter.' Families saved broken crockery to embed the brightly coloured fragments in the mountain paths so children could find their way to and from school.

'But it wasn't lonely, that was the odd thing,' said Iorwerth Davies. 'You couldn't go anywhere except to your neighbours, so people called on each other, my mother would kill a chicken, and there'd be an evening of singing and telling stories. Not everyone had a wireless, but we did, and then we had no end of people call on us.'

One old gentleman claimed he had known the wireless was coming long before it was even invented, because up there with his sheep he had heard voices in the air. When he finally did have his own set and heard people coughing, he and his wife would sit as far away from it as possible because of the risk of disease. An old lady, recalling life on the Epynt, told Herbert Hughes, 'We had the whole world to ourselves.' And it is a quote that, once read, you never forget.

It was on this small, close, traditional society, the heartland of the

Welsh rural past that, one September day in 1939, Nemesis called, carrying maps and ringed with the morning sun, for it was glorious weather. Nemesis was an Army captain in a khaki-coloured Hillman Minx driven by an ATS girl. She was blonde and beautiful, but a boy who saw her remembered chiefly the sadness of her expression. Afterwards, when the two had gone, he remembered the terrible silence of the grown-ups.

They never forgot the words the captain had used. Epynt, he said, 'would be turned into a desert for Government purposes'. Another phrase was widely quoted, of the intention 'to blast into a wilderness' the 54 farms and smallholdings. It was ideal for the purpose, the wet land precluding the danger of ricochet. They were given until the spring to make their own arrangements to go, the worst time of the year, though this was later extended to the summer because of lambing. The amount of compensation was determined by the Government.

'We were given to understand that this was on a take-it-or-leave-it basis,' said Iorwerth Davies. 'If we'd argued, we would have had nothing with which to buy another farm.' The shepherds, who did not own land, were not given any form of compensation.

By summer they were all gone, but the animals were more intractable. The Davies family of Gwybedog having found a farm 30 miles away, Iorwerth Davies had to round up their horses. 'I rode two mares into the ground before I got eighteen together and we started to walk them by road. I was riding in front, my nephew behind on a push-bike, and we thought they'd follow, but this one mare kept defying us and looking back. After we got them there she broke out one night, four others with her, but a fence stopped her. We found them 6 miles away, all of them making in a straight line for the Epynt. If the fence had been down they'd have got there.'

The Army attempted its own round-up, using three planes, fifteen tracked Bren-gun carriers and a hundred men. By the time night fell, one plane had collided with a rock, and several carriers were bogged down in the target area but, to give credit where it's due, 60 ponies and 4,000 sheep had been brought down to the valley. The only thing was, at first light most of them were back on the mountain. Later the Army, employing its finest horseman, managed, after many attempts, to capture a white stallion.

In the end some sheep were allowed to remain, otherwise the mountain would have reverted to the wild, and it is ironic that there are more sheep there now than there were in 1940. This has allowed people to revisit the mountain, said Iorwerth Davies, but many, his mother among them, could not face it. Others, a dwindling number, still come back for the annual service held by a pacifist group in the ruins of Babell chapel. But what Herbert Hughes found when he began to research his book was how many of his countrymen had forgotten what had happened. Their memories were jogged once when in 1955 the Army proposed firing long-range guns into the Epynt, which would have sent live shells over the A40 and its holiday traffic. They laid on a demonstration with a 5.5-inch gun, watched by farmers on horseback. Unfortunately, the moment the gun was fired every horse bolted, with the riders clinging on for dear life. The proposal was quietly shelved, and the Army has learnt PR skills, one of its commandants regularly attending Welsh singing festivals in the neighbouring chapels.

It is their world up there now, with their names like the Burma Road, Journey's End and Piccadilly Circus, though local people have their own names like Hellfire Pass, one of the crossings above which the red flags fly. The safety record is impressive, even though once the German motorcycle team, rehearsing for a rally, rode through the target area with guns firing all around them, a nostalgic occasion for some of the older gunners. The Senny-bridge Hunt has also materialised unexpectedly up there. But it is the cold that soldiers remember.

The Farmer and I, we watched a lorry pass, full of young men, their faces blackened for a night exercise, but under this still looking about as miserable as it is possible for human beings to look. When they come down from the Epynt it is the custom to shower first in full kit.

The Farmer laughed. 'You can see why some wouldn't want to go back,' he said.

'Would you?'

'Oh yes. When you bring sheep down off the Epynt, the old ewe wants to go back.' He looked around him at the miles of moorland, and his voice was mild.

'And the lambs?'

'The lambs won't follow.'

Roman Twilight

P ICTURE MOORLAND, a remote, barren moorland, the horizon a long way off and the sky huge. Now imagine a sunrise up there, the drums in Strauss's *Thus Spake Zarathustra* giving way to a single, unearthly trumpet. In front of you, ringed with light, is the great black monolith out of the film *2001*. It stands at the side of a road unknown to the AA, and there are no signs to indicate where this goes. But then there would have been no need of any sign: when that road was built, men knew exactly where it went. It went to Rome.

On an Ordnance Survey map, Sheet 160, find Glynneath on the A465, the Heads of the Valleys road to Merthyr. From this trace the yellow mountain road north to Ystradfellte. The green shading drains away, until where you are is just the white space and contour lines of moorland. Two and a half miles north of Ystradfellte, on your left, you will see on the map the dotted lines of the old Roman road of Sarn Helen reach the mountain road. Up there you will see nothing, not even one of those helpful brown tourist notices, just a gate, and a space in which you can park.

It is still a metalled road, but as you walk it you will see the stones put there by a local authority, or some local farmers, give way to older, much older flags, and a point will come, a quarter of a mile along, when, before a second gate, you will see the monolith start to rise, and rise, until 11 feet of it stands in the sky. On the Ordnance Survey it is marked as Maen Madoc, but that is just the name given in much later centuries when men had long forgotten what this was. In front of you is a gravestone.

And the drums are pounding.

If the light hits it at the right angle you can still make out the letters. DERVACI FILIUS IUSTI IC IACIT. (The stone of) Dervacus, Son of Justus, Here He Lies. The letters are jumbled and close together, the A's upside down, as though whoever cut these was doing his best to follow a tradition, perhaps literacy itself, only dimly remembered. No one knows who Dervacus was, or Justus, and no one will ever know. But the artist Alan Sorrell has painted an imaginative reconstruction of the raising of this stone, a little group of men and riders on the moor with the shadows lengthening as the sun goes down. Which is how it would have seemed to them. This stone was set up in a world in ruins.

2

> For the end of the world was long ago—
>   And all we dwell today
> As children of some second birth,
> Like a strange people left on earth
>   After a judgement day.

G.K. Chesterton in 'The Ballad of the White Horse' is writing about the fall of the Roman Empire, the scale of which we find hard to acknowledge. It was the nearest thing to a world state the planet has known, with a standing army and a civil service, its public buildings grander than ours, and, for the rich, villas with more comforts (the Roman room, with its couches, sideboards and underfloor heating, recreated in the Museum of London, is still the last word in comfort). For the men of the time it must have seemed all this would last forever, but it ended with an abruptness terrifying even now. Then, in Chesterton's words, there was just 'the plunging of the nations in the night'.

In the Roman world the dead had been buried beside the roads. At High Rochester, north of Hadrian's Wall, four of these tombs have been found, and they are very strange structures, big things, taller than a man, one of them circular and conical, the other three small pyramids. All were put up when the Empire stood. The difference is that the tomb on the moorland above Neath was not.

When the archaeologist Sir Cyril Fox excavated it in 1940 he found that to put it up someone had dug through the metalling of the road itself, which suggests this was overgrown even then. Roman Britain had probably been gone for two generations, with its organised life in cities and villas, and the warbands of the first English would have been picking their way through the country-side when someone decided to bury Dervacus in the old grand Imperial way. But not entirely in the old way. The Roman dead had been buried on the outskirts of towns, when, for some reason, perhaps because these towns were already ominously deserted, or for their own security, they buried him in this remote place. *The last Roman may lie here.*

3

Some 10 feet from the stone, Fox found a pit 8 feet square and 2 feet deep, the outline of which can still be seen. This was probably the grave, only there was no body. He found evidence that it had been disturbed, and this, together with the acid soil in such a high place, would have destroyed the human remains. But it is what Fox did next which is so wonderful.

The stone had fallen and was lying beside the road, but instead of carting it off to some museum, the fate of so many Roman and Dark Age memorials, he, in a time of World War with British fortunes again at their lowest, re-erected it in the old place. This is probably the most imaginative decision an archaeologist has ever taken, for it is one thing to see a stone indoors, tastefully picked out by spotlights against hessian, quite another to see it in the wind and rain where it has been for 1500 years.

So much of Roman Britain has been tidied up and set behind glass like curiosities in a china cabinet that it is hard to realise these were not just people with different kitchen inventories, they lived in what can only be described as an alternative world. This wasn't the Middle Ages, an early version of our own: this was a highly organised world, which bears comparison with ours, except their beliefs were very different. It is this *otherness* which is startling.

In Caerleon, where a Legionary fortress of 60 acres still dwarfs the modern town, you glimpse their indifference to human suffering in the great amphitheatre outside the town walls where men fought to the death. You glimpse this too in Carmarthen where an amphitheatre capable of holding 5,000 people is still the most major public space created in the town. But it can have its funny side, this otherness. In the museum at Caerleon is a small household ornament which must have stood on some sideboard, the Roman equivalent, say, of a Royal Doulton pottery Balloon Lady, except that this on any sideboard today would bring on an attack of the vapours in respectable Welsh matrons. The ornament is a carving of an erect penis, a family symbol of fertility for their equally respectable ancestors.

Still, it is when you make your own discoveries by chance that the otherness hits you. You go into the village church at Caerwent, and there in the porch is an altar not to the Christian god at all. It is to Mars, its inscription recording that a junior Roman officer had 'paid his vow willingly and duly', as though his HP payments were now complete. The Romans were very business-like in their dealings with the gods.

4

Then, in the church itself, near the lectern, you see a fragment of Roman mosaic so much more exquisite than the present stained pine floor, and, in a niche in the wall, a rare tribute to tolerance, a cremation urn which would not have been buried under Christian rites.

Some 15 miles to the north, in Lydney Park, there are remains on a hill of a pagan temple to the Celtic god Nodens. The fascinating thing about this was that it was built, not before Christianity, but in the late fourth century when Christianity was already the official religion of the Roman state. An excavation in 1804 revealed a mosaic floor, now lost, in which its dedication was recorded as being by one Titus Flavius Senilis, described as a fleet supply-depot commander, probably in a port on the Severn. So you have somebody whose job description would be familiar to civil servants in today's Ministry of Defence, who quite clearly regarded Christianity as just another religion, and a mistaken one.

On this hill has been found one of the glories of Roman art, a small bronze figure of a greyhound looking over its shoulder as though startled by something or someone: it is so life-like you feel it could at any moment leap to its feet.

Rome lingered to the west of the Severn longer than anywhere else in Britain, so that in the eighth century, 300 years after the end of Roman Britain, land was still changing hands in the language and legal forms of an empire that no longer existed. It is in the east of Britain that the great coin hoards turn up, suggesting that there the end came with terrifying suddenness, men, as they had always done in times of danger, shovelling their wealth into the earth.

So much wealth has turned up it poses another mystery: why was Britain so rich? Historians who have studied the Roman Empire all their lives cannot account for the fact that most of its treasure has been found in what, even 50 years ago, was still considered a frontier province. In 1942 a ploughman found the Mildenhall Treasure, which included the Great Dish, a silver plate of such a size he was unable to stuff it into a sack. It was four years before the authorities caught up with this, a farmer in the interval heaping fruit on it at Christmas and using silver Roman spoons to eat his puddings. At that point, of course, the puddings, and much else, hit the fan.

5

The finds in East Anglia are becoming an embarrassment. When the Hoxne Hoard *of 1500 Roman coins* was found in 1992, the first reaction of Catherine Johns, curator of the Romano-British

Collections at the British Museum, was, quite simply, 'Oh s***.' For four years ago the Museum was obliged to open a new £1.76 million gallery just to accommodate what was coming out of the ground. As its curator, Ralph Thomas, put it, 'You ask what it's like to find something like the Hoxne Hoard. I'll tell you. If we had anything on that scale again, in view of the sheer amount of work involved for us, it would be *disastrous*.'

But it is the West which is fascinating, for here you encounter not the riches of the Empire, but what Rome *meant* to men long after it had gone. I grew up in Carmarthen where behind the front door of the museum they had this huge tombstone, next to the exhibit marked, 'Dylan Thomas's cuff-links. It is believed this is the only pair ever owned by the poet.' At the time, alas, Thomas's cuff-links intrigued me more than the stone, which is the most important single thing any provincial museum has on show.

On it is written in Latin 'The monument of Votepor the Protector'. Now we know something about this Votepor: he was one of five British or Welsh kings mentioned by Gildas, the one man in sixth-century Britain to write a book, in fact the only man known to have been able to write. Gildas thought all five kings an absolute shower, but no matter. What is remarkable is that when he died, 150 years after the end of Roman Britain, the proudest title Votepor could claim was not that he had been a king, but that he had been a protector, or member of an imperial bodyguard. But there had been no imperial bodyguard, or emperor, in Britain for 150 years. It is just as though, centuries after a nuclear disaster, some local gang boss in a wasteland might still proudly be calling himself a town clerk.

The stone was found in a dingle, in the tiny church of Castelldwyran some 3 miles from Llandissilio on the A479 from Narberth to Cardigan. This is part of a farmyard now, and ducks walk through the church, but in the late nineteenth century it had its own vicar, Richard Bowen-Jones. He stole the stone and erected it in his own garden, possibly because he did not want to share top billing in a graveyard with a king. He had himself buried there in 1887 in a very grand tomb, but the vicar's son, who for some reason couldn't stand him, spoiled the effect by adding yet another one, an alternative tombstone for his father.

6

On this he had cut: 'Richard Bowen-Jones / Born 1811, Transferred 1887. / Here lie the remains of a Classical Ass / The accursed of his sons by the name of Jabrass / In the earth he is Ammonia and Triphosphate of Calcium / On earth a Home Demon and ferocious old ruffian.'

In the dingle Bowen-Jones, his boy and the old king await the Last Judgement, when they can get their hands on each other. Just as 15 miles away in the church at Steynton, near Milford Haven, a Roman called Gendilius will be waiting to get his hands on one Thomas Harries, who, when he died in 1870, had his name put on Gendilius's gravestone. The most outrageous monument in Britain is now hidden behind a pillar near the font.

But the most touching moment in this musical chairs of the graves in the west is the tombstone built into the wall of Llandissilio church, though it is centuries older than this. It had stood nearby until yet another Victorian vicar decided to use it as building material. The inscription in bad Latin and straggling capitals reads: Clutorix, son of Paulinus Marinus of Latium. Just as with Dervacus on the moor, someone had decided to bury Clutorix in the old way.

But the proudest thing they could find to say about him was

that his dad was the genuine article, having come from the Imperial heartland. It is a small and fleeting moment of snobbery in the darkness of Rome.

R.S. Thomas

H E WAS THE strangest bundle of contradictions. This was the poet who wrote of country clergymen that they were 'Toppled into the same graves / With oafs and yokels,' but was a country clergyman himself, the oafs and yokels the ancestors of his own parishioners. 'I suppose that did shock the bourgeoisie,' said R.S. Thomas.

A poem started, 'Men of the hills, wantoners, men of Wales / With your sheep and your pigs and your ponies, your sweaty females / How I have hated you…' – and the man who wrote that was such an extreme nationalist that he could not support Plaid Cymru because it recognised the English Parliament.

If he was a puzzle to his English-reading public, just think how much more so he was to his own countrymen, for this was a Holyhead man, the product of the town's schools, who spoke the English language without the trace of a Welsh accent – spoke it, in fact, with all the coldness and weariness of its own ruling class. For almost half a century he was married to an English woman, and, when I asked him once if she had not objected to his banging on about her race, he said, '*Amor vincit omnia*.' His son went to an English boarding school.

He was in *Who's Who*, but at one point that would have told you more about the private lives of the old Soviet leaders. There was a name, 'THOMAS, Ronald Stuart', followed by the reason for its inclusion — 'poet' — but, after that, just a list of church livings and of books, also an address, for he was a vicar after all. But there was no record of parents, marriage, fatherhood, not even a date of birth. In old age he relented and supplied most of these, even throwing in his Queen's Medal for Poetry but, unlike the gardening, fishing, motoring princes of his church, never did add 'recreations'. There was only one, birdwatching, and this was there in the poems — just as everything else was there in the poems.

It is the dilemma of the lyric poet that his material is his own life, his commodity intimacy. Thomas Hardy in old age sent up a smoke-screen against future biographers by guardedly writing an autobiography which he got his wife to publish after his death under her own name. R.S. Thomas wrote his in Welsh, and called it *Neb* — nobody. There was mischief in this, for the answers his admirers sought were in a language they could not understand. But it also reflected the bitterness which danced attendance on him as he grew old, that he had learnt his native language too late in life to write poetry in it. 'All those words, and me outside them.'

To adapt what someone said of De Gaulle, Thomas had one illusion, Wales, and one hate, the Welsh, who had been born into a tradition they neglected, and which he, like a tramp at Christmas, was doomed to stand outside. He said once that there had been no personal influences on his life, no guiding schoolmaster or tutor — and little contact later with anyone who could be considered his peer. He took no newspapers, entertained no friends. He was the loneliest man I ever met.

It was partly the loneliness of the country priest, cut off by his cloth and learning, but a lot more was deliberate. He felt so cut off from the modern world, with its cult of personality, that, in the autobiography, he referred to himself throughout in the third person – as 'the boy', 'RS', 'the rector' – as though watching himself, often with startled interest, from space. He could take this sense of distance to hair-raising lengths, as when, asked whether he felt lonely after the death of his wife, he said he sometimes felt lonely when she was alive. It is one thing to encounter bleak honesty in the poems, but quite another to encounter it in conversation.

'It was difficult to talk to Mr Thomas,' a reporter wrote disgruntledly. 'He makes it almost obsessively clear that he does not suffer fools, or foolish things, easily.' He would not have recognised the self-portrait of the autobiography, of a figure encased in innocence, who accommodated the ambitions and needs of others. Thomas's mother, a possessive woman, thought the priesthood a safe career: he became a priest. His wife wanted a child ('the possibility of this had not entered his mind'): the child was born, 'with his huge hunger,' wrote the poet who could also start a poem, 'Dear parents / I forgive you my life.'

He was a sea captain's son, read Latin at University College, Bangor, where he also played rugby – the forbidding initials stemmed from the team lists, which contained more than one Thomas – was ordained, and married the painter Elsi Eldridge, then an art teacher at Oswestry high school. They had one son, Gwydion, a lecturer in education, who never learnt Welsh, unlike his father, who did so at the age of 30. The relationship between Thomas and his country was a strange one. It began and ended in Holyhead, so what lay between was an odyssey – from Chirk, his first curacy, on the border, to Manafon, a border parish, to another in mid-Wales, and to the last, at Aberdaron, at the western edge of Wales. This should have been a progression into the heart of Welshness, only it wasn't; there was much black comedy in the odyssey.

Those who knew only the public figure of his later years, with his bitter pronouncements on English incomers – 'the cantankerous clergyman', 'the fiery poet-priest' – would have been startled to meet him in his beginnings, the curate trudging dutifully towards his weekly lesson with a copy of *Welsh Made Easy* under his arm. But then, there was also comedy about the later years, when, in the Welsh heartland, he met English pensioners in their holiday homes ('an Elsan culture / Threatens us'). This produced the public figure, when the press picked up the chance remark that he could understand the motives of those who burnt down these cottages.

There were many interviews then, and many photographs of a wild, gaunt face against the sky, or scowling over the half-door of the sixteenth-century cottage to which he had retired. Controversy surfaced again when he was nominated for the Nobel prize in his 82nd year, for it had been largely forgotten that this ogre was also the finest living lyric poet, ironically, in the English language.

Acclaim came late. Thomas was 42 when Rupert Hart-Davis brought out *Song At The Year's Turning*, before which there had been just one book, printed at his own expense, and a few poems in magazines. John Betjeman contributed a preface, in which he wrote, 'The name which has the honour to introduce this fine poet to a wider public will be forgotten long before that of RS Thomas.' There were some generous reviews, Kingsley Amis calling him 'one of the best half-dozen poets now writing in English', and, by the time *Selected Poems* appeared twenty years later, an anonymous reviewer in the *TLS* was starting to use words like 'major poetry'. Suddenly, nobody was making the old charge that Thomas was a 'limited' poet.

Yet it was easy to see why it had been made. He wrote about the hill farmers he had met in his first parish, a people and a way of life very few of his readers would have encountered. He wrote about religious faith, when, for many, this would have held only an historical interest. He attacked modern life, modern technology, the English encroaching into Wales and the Welsh responsible for the decay of their own culture and language.

There is no comfort in any of these poems. 'Too far for you to see / The fluke and the foot-rot and the fat maggot / Gnawing the skin from the small bones / The sheep are grazing at Bwlch-y-Fedwen, / Arranged romantically in the usual manner / On a bleak background of bald stone.' The hill farmer, at one moment a cosmic symbol of endurance, is also greedy, joyless, physically repugnant.

There is no comfort in the religious poetry either, and no answers. One, called 'Earth', begins: 'What made us think / It was yours? Because it was signed / With your blood, God of battles?' Yet there is a grim compassion for the hill farmer, and there is the odd abrupt burst of lyricism, when the poet is caught off-guard by the beauty of the natural world.

But the tone is inevitably the bleak, ruthlessly honest note Thomas had made his own. There is a hardness about his rhythms, and a clarity about his words and images ('Who put the crease in your soul, Davies?') that preserved him from the misanthropy and the ranting into which some of his attitudes could have betrayed him. Later, he added God to his dramatis personae, a cold figure indifferent to His creation, and there were small collections with titles like 'H'm', in which the main emotions seemed to be weariness and disgust. 'Just souring old age,' said Thomas. 'My mother used to ask my father, "Haven't you a good word to say about anybody?" He thought for a long time and said "No."'

But it was an industrious disgust, for he wrote on and on, and it was startling to be reminded of just how many small collections there had been when the *Collected Poems* appeared, a volume of 500 pages, of near-Victorian dimensions. In old age the poems were increasingly abstract, God increasingly absent – though much addressed – so the bursts of lyricism were winter sunlight. This is on the death of his wife:

> We met
> under a shower
> Of bird-notes.
> Fifty years passed,
> love's moment
> in a world in
> servitude to time.
> She was young;
> I kissed with my eyes
> closed and opened
> them on her wrinkles.
> 'Come,' said death,
> choosing her as his
> partner for
> the last dance. And she,
> who in life
> had done everything
> with a bird's grace,
> opened her bill now
> for the shedding
> of one sigh no
> heavier than a feather.

I met him when I was seventeen. He suggested we had tea in a hotel on the seafront at Aberystwyth, but in summer there are many clerical collars in Aberystwyth. A fat man in specs passed, and I hoped it would not be him, then a cheerful chap with a pipe, and I hoped it would not be him either. But then a third man came, a tall, lean athletic man bent against the wind – and it was the face of the poems. When I wrote about it later, I used adjectives like 'hard' and 'severe', and had the phrase 'almost predatory'. By return of post came a letter from Thomas, in which he signed himself 'Nimrod'. That sense of humour, faint and dry, and so baffling to the young, was the strangest of all his contradictions.

Moments

Who Wrote This Stuff?

THE ASSISTANT PRIVATE SECRETARY'S embarrassment was evident, even on the telephone. Oliver Everett, a civil servant transferred to the Prince of Wales's Office (and a 'high-flier' according to a Press which has yet to identify a low-flier in the Civil Service), had always been careful of speech to the point where you fancied you saw semicolons form in air. But this time he sounded as though English were a foreign language in which he was taking an oral exam.

'It's about the... er, speeches. D'you think... umm... it might be... possible... for you... to stop using the first person singular? I've been asked to pass this on. In future, could you... umm... remember to use HRH?'

'You mean, I have to remind myself I am not the Prince of Wales,' I said helpfully.

'You could put it like that, yes.'

Pronouns were always a bit of a problem. Until the late 20th century, royalty moved in a narrow social group, the members of which had been schooled in the old ways of deference. Royalty was 'ma'am' and 'sir', and I can remember Lady Jane Wellesley telling me that she had never called the Prince of Wales anything but 'sir', which struck me then, and still does, as one of the saddest little confessions I have ever heard. It did not matter that royalty, ambitious to involve itself in social issues, found itself increasingly among people who had never called anyone 'sir' in their lives. Royalty was secretly a stickler for the old forms. The first greeting of the day, I had been informed, was to be 'your Royal Highness', thereafter 'sir'. It was hard to keep this up in conversations.

'Who was this Aleister Crowley?'

'Wickedest Man in the World... sir.'

What complicated things even more was that royalty when it signed letters (which always came by Registered Post) did so with a single Christian name, which suggested an intimacy that never was. It is only on marriage certificates that royalty has a surname, and even then it is a matter of debate as to what this is.

Sighing, I pulled towards me the draft of a speech to be delivered to the Highland Society. 'It is a matter of some poignance that I should address a society formed because one member of the family raised the clans and another blew them to bits in 30 minutes flat...'. I began to change the pronouns.

It had all started late one summer's night when the phone rang. The caller was a man I had not spoken to for thirteen years, ever since he was the editor of the *Sheffield Star* and I a graduate trainee. Since then, Tom Watson had become a director of United Newspapers, at the time a chain of provincial papers which also included the *Observer* and *Punch*. I was then a freelance journalist in London, and, as we talked, I kept wondering how he had managed to get hold of my home number.

Tom was affability itself, chatting on about people we both knew, before saying, could I give Lord Barnetson a ring? Barnetson was a mysterious figure, a press lord about whom nobody knew much except that he was chairman of United Newspapers, of Reuters and of just about everything else. What was I to ring him about? Tom was suddenly vague, suggesting that perhaps a letter might be better. But what was I to say in this letter? Oh nothing much, just that my old editor had suggested I write. He then chuckled and rang off.

I was 35 years old, unmarried, and a few minutes earlier had been sitting in a chair wondering whether to go out for a drink or to bed. I found myself thinking about the novels of John Buchan, which often started as quietly as that, and the next moment you were in full flight across a moor. As a freelance I thought I should welcome the moor, or anything else which would rescue me from the blank paper and the loneliness. A few days later I wrote to Barnetson. His secretary rang back, first to arrange an interview, then a second time to ask for a curriculum vitae, which I grumpily sent.

It rained the day of the interview and I was soaked by the time I got to the United Newspapers offices behind Fleet Street, where a doorman was waiting for me. He showed me to a lift, which went up all of one floor to where a secretary was also waiting. Philip Marlowe would have wisecracked his way through this; I followed her, clutching my cycle clips the way a child holds a comforter. She showed me into a boardroom dominated by a large oil painting of Barnetson, a man with a small moustache and hooded eyes, smoking a pipe. A door opened and a smaller version of the painting came in, who smoked his pipe and looked at me; he seemed at ease in silence.

And he made all this inconsequential chat, talking, bizarrely enough, about John Buchan (whose election agent he had once been), so that I began to think, what with him and Watson, there were either a lot of men who had time on their hands or were lonely. But then he laid his pipe down. He had some questions to ask, he said. Was I interested in politics? No, I said. Had I ever written for *Private Eye*? No, I lied. And that was it.

He began to talk about something he referred to as 'this position', which was, he said, to write speeches for a public figure. No, not for him; he was a mere go-between, but whoever took 'this position' would find himself a shoulder for an unnamed man to lean on. He could not say more, but this would involve meeting prominent men, a consummation, he implied, devoutly to be wished. There might be a book in it, he said, showing me to the door, suddenly the young hack again with his way to make.

But what could the man be? Not a politician, not a captain of industry, for these were thick as thieves with journalists. It had to be someone who, despite being famous, was isolated and, from Barnetson's remarks, vulnerable. There came a point when I began to suspect where these trails converged and I remembered the very young face I had seen eight years before, beyond a scrum of journalists at Aberystwyth, but that seemed absurd. Why me?

A week went by, two weeks. I rang Barnetson. He laughed and said I would have to get used to the pace at which this group of people operated. Yes, it was Charles, he said, and the next thing would be lunch with his Private Secretary, David (now Sir David) Checketts.

In the 1970s, you must remember, royalty was the most secret and mysterious force in society. Biographers kept their distance then, and opponents such as the MP Willie Hamilton regarded it as a regressive but horribly efficient piece of machinery at the centre of things. Yet nobody really knew how royalty operated: it was like an unexplored galaxy, and here I was among its outer rings, my journey just beginning. What would I find at the end? Would I be Buckingham to the Prince's Charles I?

Barnetson arranged a lunch at the Savoy Grill. Checketts was late. Barnetson sat wreathed in pipe smoke and nodding to famous men. 'Hello, Harry,' he said, and then to me, 'That was Chapman Pincher.' Then Checketts came. 'Big boy, aren't you,' he said as I stood to shake hands. I remembered him from Aberystwyth during that bizarre term when the Prince was given a crash course there in the Welsh language. Checketts had seemed then like one of nature's gym masters, forceful, tough, not over troubled by humour.

Over lunch he and Barnetson talked about their country houses while I ate everything on the table, feeling like the Dormouse at the Mad Hatter's Tea Party. But when the coffee came Checketts turned abruptly to me and began to talk about what he called 'a possible role'. No mention of shoulders now. If things worked out I would be a machine, just as he was a machine, for when he outlived his uses even he would be gone. There were no pension rights in his job, volunteered Checketts. He would like to say a few words about what the Prince actually did. A few months before, he said solemnly, he had lent his name to a campaign to have bicycle theft stamped out in Cornwall, and was also passionately interested in having old canals re-dug. Barnetson's vision of great events was crashing about my ears as Checketts got to his feet. The next step, he said briskly, was to meet the Boss, 'to see whether the chemistry worked'.

That was August. A month went by. I dropped a note to Checketts saying the chemistry practical seemed to be taking an awfully long time to arrange. The letter from Checketts contained no jokes; the earliest possible time was in October, he wrote, and somehow contrived to give the impression that it was I who was seeking the interview.

I cycled to the Palace on an autumn morning. There were still a few tourists at the gates. They looked at me curiously as the policeman on duty scanned a list of names and pointed me towards the Privy Purse door, the right wing of the façade. I was finally inside. A sentry's boots crashed into the gravel as he turned a few yards from where I crouched, chaining up my bike, for old habits died hard and bicycle theft figured large in my mind.

A man in a tailcoat was expecting me and I sat under Frith's Derby Day (there are no prints in the Palace) as he phoned through. There was no sign of a living soul as I was directed across the inner courtyard to the Prince's offices. I was nearing the centre of the galaxy. Which, incredibly, was a line of luggage as far as the eye could see, enough to equip a battalion for embarkation, except that each case, each hat box, bore the three feathers. That was the first shock, for the Jubilee was just over and I had read many articles on the Monarchy as a force in the modern world, yet here was the sort of kit an eighteenth-century aristocrat would take on a Grand Tour.

That was all. This time there was nobody waiting for me. In the end I knocked at a door and the young man who appeared seemed pleased at the interruption, any interruption. He was an army officer, the Prince's military equerry, and took me to Checketts, who occupied a large office opposite. This looked like an Oxford don's sitting room except that there was a large black Labrador asleep on the floor. Checketts rang through and we walked to an old lift which took us to the second floor. He raised one finger, knocked on a door and disappeared as suddenly as the White Rabbit.

I was left among the red and gold, red carpets, gold framed oil paintings almost touching, and a decor which could have been by the man responsible for Gaumont cinema foyers. The sheer amount of stuff on display was remarkable; come the revolution, someone could go out of his mind trying to produce an inventory of Buckingham Palace. My journey was ending. Like Pompey, I was about to enter the Holy of Holies.

The door opened and I went in. More oil paintings, more reds, more gold, a leather-topped desk and the Prince of Wales coming round from behind it. He was wearing a double-breasted blazer with bright brass buttons. He looked startlingly like his photographs, only smaller. A high colour and good features, which nevertheless looked as though they had been assembled in a hurry, from memory. What I remember most is the hand I shook which was completely at odds with the rest of him; it was massive and strong, and my own hand disappeared into it.

It was a very peculiar job interview. My prospective employer seemed ill at ease, licked his lips a lot, played with a signet ring, and kept giving those eerie social smiles where the eyes wrinkle a fraction of a second before the mouth moves. It was I who asked the questions. Did he see it as a full-time job? No, part-time. Was he looking for a researcher or, I searched for the word, a phrase-maker? A researcher, said the Prince: he would write his own final drafts. But the curious thing was that Checketts introduced me to other members of the staff as the new phrase-maker. Phrase-maker. Rain-maker.

But little of this registered at the time for the Prince kept saying the strangest things. He said he was not an ambitious man. All people seemed to want, he said gloomily, was to see him; as far as speeches went, it was of no matter what the content was. There was a marked melancholy in everything he said. He found it hard to remember faces, and people became so annoyed at this for they forgot how many faces he saw. Asked whether he was looking forward to America, he said no, not really; that he made it a practice not to look forward to anything, so that anything, if it happened, could surprise him. And then he said the strangest thing of all.

The bands were playing outside the window when the Heir to the Throne informed a man he had only just met that, up until the year before, he had not believed in the Monarchy. I looked across at Checketts but he was examining the backs of his hands. It was the public response to the Jubilee which had changed his mind for him, the Prince went on, and the way crowds of people had greeted him and the Queen. He now felt the Monarchy had a function.

Checketts got to his feet. Downstairs he introduced me to Michael Colborne, the Secretary as he called him. I had expected to find an office run by tall public school men and here was a man who was a dead ringer for the Cockney comedy actor Alfie Bass. Colborne had been a petty officer on the Prince's first ship when, to his own bewilderment, he had been whisked out of the navy overnight. I liked Colborne. He seemed to have trouble with reality as well. After Checketts had gone, he told me mischievously that, contrary to appearance, he, Colborne, ran this place, then roared with laughter. He had even written some speeches, and when the Prince opened a sewage farm had contributed the fact that the average British family produced 30 pounds of the stuff a week. He had felt proud, he told me, when he heard the Prince actually say this.

I cycled thoughtfully back along the Mall, my mind full of the story of Pompey who, when he finally penetrated the Holy of Holies, had found nothing there at all. Everyone to do with the job, except the man at the centre of it, seemed so happy I felt I was about to become part of a pleasant situation comedy. No one had mentioned any of the problems associated with what a constitutional monarch-in-waiting could, or could not, say in public. As I went under Admiralty Arch, I remembered that not one of them had mentioned money either.

The story broke in the Londoner's Diary of the *Evening Standard*. 'Charles Takes On the Son of a Carpenter.' My wife, finding the cutting the other day, said this made it sound as though the Second Coming had been at hand in England in November 1977.

'Prince Charles has taken on an aide to help him with his speeches. Until now everything he had said in public has been all his own work, but in future he will be able to call on the services of Byron Rogers. Rogers is a freelance journalist from humble Welsh origins – his father was a carpenter – and his engagement by Prince Charles indicates the change in attitude at Buckingham Palace. There is now, I understand, a determination that some appointments should be made among those of lowlier stock.'

I read on, entranced. The writer, whom I knew, would clearly have had no trouble in describing the Virgin Mary as upwardly mobile. I had in fact pleaded with her on the phone not to use this particular story, but even the pleading, I noted, had been incorporated into it. Odd lot, the English: the snobbery, like damp, always shows somewhere.

The Times speculated about the nature of the job ('part-time rhetorical consultant and teller of shaggy-dog stories'), while the *Evening News* burbled about 'an unprecedented honour' (I was writing for the *News* at the time). The *Telegraph* gave it the full treatment it reserves for truly mysterious events like the death of the Glastonbury Thorn: one paragraph. 'The Prince of Wales has appointed as speech writer Mr Byron Rogers, a colourful

Welshman', as though a colourful Welshman was a job, like a bus
driver.

'I don't think it is generally known that Britain is self sufficient in
blackcurrants.' It was a month later, and I sat up in the bath, startled by the familiarity of those words. The voice was even more
familiar. I had switched on the radio, forgetting that until 7.00
on a Saturday morning at that time Radio 4 had a farming
programme.

'In fact we lead the world in the production of blackcurrants.
No imports disturb our trade figures, no foreign price rises
threaten our economy ... Every year the wind blows through
10,000 acres of British blackcurrants...'. The Prince's timing, I
noted, was very good.

The speech to the Farmers' Club was the first I had worked on,
and it set the pattern. The Palace, usually Michael Colborne,
would ring to tell me where the speech would be made, to whom
and under what circumstances. This was to be an after-dinner
speech at a Club Dinner; but the themes and the character of the
speech were left entirely to me. At one point I wrote to the Prince,
complaining that I felt like a duck-gun being pointed in an
approximate direction in the hope that the scatter pattern might
hit something, anything. He wrote back and said the duck-gun
appeared to be working.

It meant I had to rely on my wits even more than I did as a
journalist. For the Farmers' Club meeting in St James, what was
I to write about, the Common Agricultural Policy? I went to
see the Club's officers, read through a Club history (from which
I extracted the little gem that the last Prince of Wales to
address them had done so in 1923 'to an unceasing chorus of
cheers and applause, saying, it is sad to relate ... nothing whatever

of substance or importance.'). This appealed to my employer's sense of melancholy and the little quote turned up in other speeches.

But then I remembered that odd fact about the blackcurrants, tucked away somewhere at the back of my mind, and I was up and running. The rest followed, with the irony of an agricultural club in the middle of London, which in the past had been addressed on such subjects like 'Slurry'.

From the start I was aware of the comedy involved in writing speeches to be delivered in places I had never been, to men I would never meet, about matters of which I knew absolutely nothing. It was worse for my employer who had to go to those places and meet those men, but I had been hired, a member of his staff told me, to stop him starting speeches along the lines of 'Ladies and gentleman, what on earth am I doing here?', for the ladies and gentleman knew exactly what he was doing there.

So time passed. The Anglo-Venezuelan Chamber of Commerce at Caracas. The Burma Star Association. And, the ultimate unreality, something that had me walking round the room touching the furniture, an address to a gathering of engineers at Zurich University. I stole a column about engineers from my colleague Peter Simple, in whose fantasies I by then believed I had taken up residence.

I fell back on my own experiences, which then of course became the Prince's, and he would come out with anecdotes like this: 'A friend of mine was doing market research on the brewers.' Could the Prince of Wales have ever had a friend doing market research on brewers? The man had had to find the lowest social category of all so he went into a municipal garden and met a tramp. He got him into a pub, bought him a pint and the tramp opened like a rose. What did he think of Charrington's? Oh, very good. Marston's? Wonderful. But surely, my friend asked, there was some brewer he objected to? The tramp got to his feet. 'You see in front of you someone who once had a family, a job, a future. You see in front of you a man brought down by Bass.'

If the Prince's speeches ever get published, scholars may ponder over a period in his life when Welsh headmasters confided in him about the relaxed entrance requirements of the new polytechnics ('If you've anybody there who's not yet fixed up, just send him along'), and when he could describe eighteenth-century Highland society as 'the Masai, grown white and articulate, at the end of the Great North Road'.

This last remark was dropped, without preamble, into a speech, for it was the Prince's method to use a paragraph here and there (he still liked his 'What on earth am I doing here?' openings). There were of course things the Prince felt he could not say. He presided at a Press awards ceremony and I wanted him to end the speech by looking quizzically around him. 'But I see only a section of the British press in front of me, and the more poorly paid section at that. Ladies and gentlemen, where is the Linotype Operator of the Year?' His father, he said later, had raised no objection to this but the event's organisers had. I also wanted him to poke fun at his future biographer, Anthony Holden, by saying that his own job was bad enough, 'without my Boswell padding behind me in the Economy Section', but he chose instead to be nice to Holden; his attitude changed dramatically when the book appeared. He later showed me a second book written by Holden at the time of the royal marriage. Inside there was a fulsome handwritten inscription in, I think, green biro, at which he pulled a face. But the Press speech he enjoyed, especially an elaborate conceit I had worked out in which he compared his presence at such an event to a pheasant handing out prizes after a shoot.

Only once did the shit hit the fan, and that ironically was the one occasion on which I had really done some research. It was on British industry and I used the comments of American and Japanese businessmen I had interviewed on the stultifying social divide they had seen here between the executive restaurant and the works canteen. The Prince made the speech, and that night on the television news I listened to something extraordinary, a CBI spokesman denouncing a member of the Royal Family. Even more extraordinary, I met that weekend in the pubs of Carmarthen working men who remembered the comments of Edward VIII in the Rhondda and felt that they might again have a prince who understood.

The question of payment took months to work out, and required a meeting with Checketts, who in a memo had said, 'I rather thought he [Rogers] was going to do this work for nothing.' They were not quite of the modern world, these men, and I remembered the remarks of one member of staff when the Prince, attempting to intervene in the social problems of south London, called a conference of police officers and black teenagers at the Palace. 'They all came but at a certain time HRH got up and said, "Well, I'm afraid I have to go now." Which left all these policemen and teenagers staring at each other round a table in Buckingham Palace.'

Checketts asked what was the going rate in journalism, and I, plucking a figure out of the air, suggested £125 per thousand words. That worked for a while except that if something interested me I wrote on. And on. Oliver Everett, newly transferred from the Foreign Office, then came up with an impeccable Civil Service compromise: the grading of speeches according to their public importance, fees to range from £65 for a post-prandial jolly to £125 for Sermons on the Mount. I could of course have stealthily trebled this, as Mr James Whittaker suggested one night at a reception; it only required a phone call, said Mr Whittaker, scribbling a number on a piece of paper. I never did, not only out of loyalty – the reality of life beyond those gates was just too bizarre.

A remarkable young man, more camp than Julian Clary, minced into Michael Colborne's office. When he had gone I asked who he was, for Colborne, I noticed, had not introduced us. 'That,' he said heavily, 'is the best reason for getting the Prince of Wales married as soon as possible.' It had been the Prince's valet. On another occasion I walked in to find Colborne's desk covered in knitted woollen socks; someone had called, hoping to get a Royal Warrant.

The Palace itself, like everything else, was not what it seemed. Entered from the Mall it was a Palace, but entered from the side, the Buckingham Gate entrance, it was a DoE storehouse, with men wheeling trolleys and a notice-board on which the footmen tried to sell each other second-hand cars (the Chaplain's Rover was at one point up for sale). But then you went through a door, the carpet started, and you were in the Palace again.

There were so many corridors on so many different levels that occasionally I lost my way, and once, below ground, came on a door marked 'Royal Clockmaker', which I could never find afterwards. Below ground I saw people going about their jobs, but above not a soul, so if you kept your nerve you could wander at will. Once I surfaced in the Throne Room.

There was the odd social event, like the Ball before the Wedding at which I saw the bride-to-be run across the room like a hunted thing. The guests were remarkable – the Cabinet talking warily to each other, foreign royalty in strange uniforms, two of the Goons, and Mrs Nancy Reagan. Nobody, I noted, awaited her at the door, so the Empress of the West entered very small and alone.

Some guests got extremely plastered, for there was a bar serving the strongest cocktails I have ever drunk. I caught one tiny dowager as she fell down the main stairs and she weighed no more than a piece of cardboard; her make-up, close to, was pale green, like that of one of Dracula's Brides. At the cocktail bar a huge bull in scarlet turned to me. 'No finer sight in the world than a good Catholic girl with hair under her arms, dontcha think?' Up to a point, I said.

How did it end? My wife was asking me that the other night, and all I could tell her was that, just as in Hollywood, the phone stopped ringing. I was not sad because the Engineers' Speech in Switzerland represented a final marker of lunacy for a man who had never met an engineer in his life. But there was no final letter of thanks, not even a row, nothing at all after five years. My own idea, for what it is worth (God, I am even beginning to sound like the Prince in the speeches he was then making) was that an article may have contributed. It had become known that I was doing this work so editors had been keen on getting me to write about royalty. I turned them down but the idea of writing an open letter to the new Princess of Wales in the *Telegraph* Magazine intrigued me.

'People will talk about you endlessly, about your appearance and your imagined relationships with other members of the Family. In some households you will be like a relative who never calls...'. It was kindly meant, and Colborne told me it had been much appreciated. But then I wrote for the *Express* an open letter to the infant Prince William (and probably would have gone on writing open letters to all of them, down to the corgis), and halfway through this quoted two paragraphs from a ninth-century biography of the Emperor Charlemagne. The writer is describing the lot of the earlier Merovingian kings of France.

'Nothing was left the king except the name of king ... He sat on his throne and played at government, gave audience to envoys, and dismissed them with answers he had been schooled, or rather commanded, to give. He had nothing to call his own except one estate ... and a not very numerous retinue. He travelled when occasions required it in a wagon drawn by oxen ... in this guise he came to the palace or to the annual assembly of his people. The mayor of the palace controlled the administration and decided all issues of policy at home and abroad...'. The parallels were remarkable and I helpfully spelt them out at length, even to the State Coach.

'You must have been completely off your rocker if you thought you could go on writing speeches for royalty after that,' said my wife.

The last time I saw the Prince was at Highgrove, where he seemed happy. We talked about the DIY he was doing, and Nitromors, and a piece of celebrated modern furniture which he had quietly relegated to his detective's room. I also met an old Irishman he was fond of, a character Colborne told me would make a funny profile. It is sad to read about what has happened after. The prince gave me a piece of cake to take away, and I never saw him again.

Nude

SEE HER NOW as I shall always see her, standing in that long Georgian window in the morning sun. She is not looking out. In fifteen years, I saw her look out only once and then, like the Lady of Shalott, she was startled into doing so. The rest of the time she just stood there, drying her hair. She is, of course, nude. She was always nude.

It was the athlete's body of a natural blonde, long of thigh and neat of bust. And at 8.00 every morning it stood there, across gardens the length of two cricket pitches which separated us. My flat in Islington faced west, hers east, and I shall never forget her. You could say we grew old together.

I moved to the country but kept the flat on, and however long I had been away I would always look out of the window on my return and there she would be at 8.00 a.m., wrapping a towel round her head and flicking the ends over one broad shoulder. It became one of the certainties of my life.

She must have been about 25 when I first saw her, which would have made her 40 towards the end, but the years were not unkind, though this might have been a tribute to the attention she lavished on her body. As someone said of Robespierre, he was busy every day of his life. And she was busy. That daily half-hour in the window was like landscape gardening to her, with her body the landscape. It couldn't have been exhibitionism; she was too engrossed in what she was about. She was there at her most vulnerable, before the make-up went on, and make-up meant a lot to her. No astronaut prepared himself for space the way she did for the office.

When I saw her first it was a June morning and the sun was full on her; I thought it the most erotic sight I had ever seen and felt guilty. Anyone who has lived in London will have seen something like this once or twice, but she was there again the next day, and the next, so obsession replaced guilt. It got to the point where one morning, seeing her about to go out, I rushed outside and we collided in the street. She was very tall, not beautiful – her face had that bleached, expressionless look of some Scandinavian women. I said, 'Sorry' and she gave a tight little smile. We never met again.

The American filmmaker James Hill, producer of *The Sweet Smell of Success*, was staying with me at that time and the situation intrigued him. He saw it as a short film and kept dreaming up scripts, but each of these, in true Hollywood fashion, had a resolution. They required me to meet her. I wasn't keen on this. I mean, what would my first words have been? 'You won't know me, but I feel I know you very well'? Slam. 'I live opposite and every morning I see you in your window'? Smack. In the end Hill agreed. 'Guess we'll have to work on this one.' But we never did.

Besides, the relationship had moved on. Familiarity buried the obsession and the morning came when I realised I was looking at that body with the lack of interest of an old, married man. Yet I was proud of it in a distant way, and it puzzled me that she should always be alone. Then that too changed, for one morning, ten years after I first saw her, there was a man there — a big, fat chap with a moustache. For the few months he was there I was sad, for I felt he was not good enough for her, my Diana in the Georgian window.

I got married about this time and when my wife stayed in the flat I told her about this lady. As if on cue, she appeared at that moment. My wife, whose eyesight is not good, leaned out, the curtains blowing behind her, and that was the only time the Lady of Shalott looked out. A blind I had never seen before was hastily pulled down, but the next week it was up again.

I don't know when she left her flat. All I know is that a week ago I looked across and there was someone else there. A stocky brunette stood shamelessly in the window, naked as a penny piece. And I closed the curtains.

When a Young Man's Dreams Expire

A MOMENT OF SOCIAL HISTORY. It was Sunday morning, just after breakfast, in the junior common room of an Oxford college deserted except for two men, both middle-aged and moving with edgy stateliness, for this was the morning after the night before. They had stopped in front of a long metal box fixed at chest-level to the wall; there was no other form of ornament, so the box dominated not only the wall but the whole room.

'Incredible,' said one of them, a northern GP, shaking his head. 'I mean, what sort of people are these, for God's sake? Can you imagine going anywhere near that thing with everyone looking?'

I should add that this was once a man very active in that particular direction, who never lost his nerve in chemist shops like the rest of us and bought Horlicks tablets. Now, 30 years on and up for a college reunion, we were staring at the contraceptive machine as though we had come on some terrible tribal juju in a jungle clearing.

'So they've had it put up at last,' said the retired don, with weariness in his voice. It was now noon, the sherry hour. 'Twenty years ago, that was one of the great confrontations of my time. The Dean refused point blank, which was a mistake. The matter went to a committee and then to a meeting of the fellows. They asked the Chaplain for guidance but he talked about the moral responsibility of the undergraduates. We were running scared, they were so militant.' 'And then?' 'Oh then, there were the holidays,' he chuckled. 'By the time they came back the undergraduates had forgotten all about the thing. Of course, this was after your time.'

My time... The 100 men who met that weekend have probably never been so conscious of time. It was a great shock for a man to go back, Dr Johnson said towards the end of his life. He had gone back to Lichfield, where he had met men who were boys when he was a boy and, seeing they were now old, it had occurred to him he was old too. Some of these men were old.

We met at tea in the Master's Lodge on Saturday afternoon, walking round and round each other like strange dogs and talking loudly to dispel the thin wind of mortality we must all have felt. Men who had lived on the same staircase failed to recognise each other, and one man had to introduce himself to his former roommate. The average age must have been around 50, yet one man said he was reminded of a station on one of those days when British Rail offered concessionary fares to pensioners. And then a face appeared with all the woes of the world upon it, these being his stock in trade: the newsreader had arrived.

There were bankers, lawyers, doctors, academics, men who had lost themselves to careers or tried to find themselves on Scottish islands, who, in the intervening decades had discovered God or homosexuality or wives. And now for this weekend all these were offstage.

Why had they come? Nostalgia, curiosity, the chance to swank

or merely the opportunity of a free meal? Perhaps it was in search
of the most mysterious being anyone will encounter, the man he
himself once was. He survives in photographs, in suits which no
longer fit, in things he wrote. You know everything about your
varnished self but in a biographer's way; if the man you once were
came through the door, you might not even recognise him.

'Remember the time you went to see the doctor because you
thought your nipples were different sizes?' I asked a Doctor of
Philosophy, trying to break the ice.

'I've learnt to keep secrets now,' he said. 'This will be a disappointment to you.'

Some men talked about their children and one about his
impending divorce ('No, don't sympathise, I've been planning
this'). He looked so happy and so young I began to suspect there
might be a correlation between youth and a bad marital track
record.

The head of Scotland Yard's Forensic Science Laboratory
scribbled his phone number on a piece of paper and gave it to me
('Now be careful what you do with that'). I reproached a
stipendiary who, when I appeared in front of him on a motoring
charge (with a discreet little wave), had promptly disqualified
himself from hearing the case.

'You could have got me off.'

'You were pleading guilty, you fool.'

'Oh yes, so I was, but you could have done something.'

'And what do you think the Lord Chancellor would have done
to my career then?'

The old Head Porter, treasured by generations for his unblink-
ing range of obscenity, held court, while the Master, who did not
recognise anyone, kept materialising uneasily in various parts of
his parlour like Doctor Who.

Many had flown to be there. I shook hands with one of those clear-eyed Americans who look out of place anywhere except on the Great Plains.

'So what do you do?' I asked.

'I own newspapers.'

'How many do you own?'

'Fifty.'

'Do you really... sir?'

And it was time to change for dinner. I called on an old friend and a head came round the door. 'Oh it's you, come in.' he said. He was in his vest. 'I don't mind you seeing my stick-like arms.' Ah yes, the stick-like arms, once as familiar as a piece of heraldry; he had spent most of our three years together tuning self-deprecation until this was an art form. It was strange. With others it had been like members of some trade delegation meeting, but with him, families and careers were irrelevant and we were again the silly young men we had once been. We walked to the pub.

As I ordered drinks, I overheard an extraordinary conversation. The two men at the bar, both in dinner jackets, were talking intently. 'You remember Watkins then, surely he was your year?' 'No, but Jim Hill was.' 'Never heard of him. What about Highcock?' 'Didn't know anyone by that name. Chris Horne?' 'No.'

The litany went on and on, each man looking more and more bewildered as it became clear they did not have a single acquaintance in common. I was sitting down when there was a sudden roar of laughter from the bar, and after one had left, still laughing, the other joined us.

'God,' he said. 'That was terrible. That chap made me feel older than Rip van Winkle. He kept telling me names and I couldn't remember any of them. But then it turned out he was up for a different reunion; he wasn't at our College at all.'

Over dinner in Hall the Master reproached us for not being sufficiently rich and famous. I had forgotten how much worldly success meant to dons. When the present head of the Civil Service returned to college, whispered someone, his testicles were supported on a velvet cushion held by the Head Porter. Reproaches over, the Master got down to the serious business of fundraising. Old members' contributions, he declared, had so far made possible a Fellowship in English Literature. 'Stand up.' And the Eng. Lit. don, a small bearded man, stood. His contribution to the College was enormous, said the Master relentlessly; his lectures on structuralism were guaranteed to put anyone to sleep.

In my time the College had no female undergraduates, but these were now waiting on us, having spent much of the long vac waiting on various conferences. Some wore black stockings, others no stockings at all, and their skirts were short. One girl was beautiful. 'They must be wondering who all these old farts are,' I told my neighbour. 'Perhaps not,' he said. 'Perhaps they're thinking, "It's all very well, young men with beautiful bodies. Perhaps some of those old boys have real feelings."'

I knew he was wrong when the beautiful waitress went by and awarded me the brisk, unfocused smile of a vicar's wife. Over brandy the stipendiary gave me a cigar ('Perhaps you'll shut up now'). Some men grew confidential in drink, one telling me he had thought of committing suicide when we were up, which stunned me, for he had been such a cheerful man and played rugby. In others, the ugliness of an all-male society surfaced.

One man told another he had subsequently employed his former girlfriend. 'So I know all about you.' 'Do you really?' 'Yes, and I bet you had a good time there, didn't you?' 'You do know she's dead.' 'Of course I know she's dead.'

After breakfast I met a man with his bags packed outside the

Porter's Lodge. 'I can't take anymore of this,' he said. 'I was sitting in Hall just now and for a moment I felt the familiarity of everything. I knew that panelling, those pictures. Then I looked around me and saw faces I didn't know at all. It was like a horror story.'

And what Phillip Larkin called 'this frail travelling coincidence' was almost over. I walked down the high street and met the head of Scotland Yard's Forensic Science Lab squirting oil on to the leads of a car which had failed to start. 'We must have lunch,' he said vaguely.

Singles Weekend

T O BEGIN WITH IT was like starting a new school. We inspected each other at a distance, did not speak, looked away when eyes just as full of curiosity, speculation, suspicion met our own. There is great wariness at the start of a Singles Weekend.

I have spread my dreams under your feet.
Tread softly, for you tread on my dreams.

Playwrights from that lost age when plays had plots would have boggled at the good fortune of it: there we were, 25 strangers come together in a Cotswolds hotel. It was not the reading of a will that had brought us there, nor a snowstorm that detained us, but the outside world dropped away as remorselessly as a shoreline. For a weekend we were left with each other, and our dreams.

All we had in common was loneliness and the ability to cough up the sum required, for the organisers, like the writers of romantic fiction, believed in putting obstacles in the way of True Love. The first was cost. The second was inconvenience, for they did not believe in romantic locations. The Singlers must struggle in Nottingham and Darlington and, even, in the inspired lunacy of An All-Night Party In The English Channel In October, and not all the wicked uncles and mistaken identities in the world can compete with that one. If, in a Dover dawn, draped over the rails like old towels, your eyes still meet, then True Happiness must be yours.

All weekends were advertised in the monthly *Select* magazine, weekends, magazine and a computer dating agency being part of the same company. The magazine was amiable enough, though given to denunciations of masturbation as severe as in any Victorian handbook on youth. It was only afterwards you appreciated the commercial logic of this: a booming industry needs to knock out competition.

Anyway there we were, newly arrived in the lounge bar, wondering which were ordinary hotel guests and which Singles. Spy rings meeting for the first time are probably like this. But in addition there was embarrassment: was it social failure that led to this confrontation in the hills? There was also a small fluttering even in the most threadbare soul. What if she did turn up, the blonde with the long legs who could fill in tax forms and fix car engines? Help!

I had read with mounting awe the five pages of lonely hearts advertisements which concluded the *Select* magazine. At no time, unless it was the Hollywood of the 1930s, could more eligible people have assembled in one place. There were merchant bankers and film producers, men with Bentleys, men with country houses. There were men who knew their hearts' desire so precisely they even knew its poundage, 'under 140 pounds, laconic, lovable and lusty'. There was what might have been a misprint, 'a slightly older man, educated, king'. Some were boastful, some were smug; some hid their feelings under bravado ('I dare you...'). But one was urgent, 'for any female, any age'. Another said, simply, 'I am 21 and tired of being on my own.' One showed the accents of experience: 'No philanderers or fusspots, please.'

The weekend did not begin well. My roommate, a young solicitor from the North, lay glumly on his bed with his golf clubs around him. The hotel course, so beautifully photographed in the brochure, had been closed. He was cross, he said, because he had allowed this to surprise him. From his first Singles Weekend he remembered the lack of organisation and the fact that the Singlers, like Victorian domestics, had been obliged to eat from a different menu to the rest of the guests. Defiantly he had arranged his aftershave lotions and deodorants under the bathroom mirror: bored he might have to be, but smell like a human being he would not. It was the same organiser this time as last, came a mournful voice from the bedroom.

We met, as arranged, in the bar downstairs just before dinner. We were given one free glass of wine each. Now I had always thought I could drink anything, but the red wine I was given at the Hotel de la Bere near Cheltenham was off all gastronomic maps. Yet the Singlers drank it. The men stood silently by the bar, and the women, in long dresses, sat together. We had the nervousness of teenagers, though few of us would ever see 40 again (and even fewer would want to, with wine like that in the world). We were 25 in number, teachers, accountants, farmers, lab technicians. There were just three under 30, and at least one over 60, and we were as uncomfortable as anyone at a school dance. Perhaps that was why we were there. Certainly nothing but nerves could account for the fact that we were actually drinking the wine.

The organiser (or host, as the programme called him) was a

very thin young man who came and went during the weekend like
the White Rabbit. He made no introductions, and spoke to very
few of us. Most of the time he hovered on the fringes as though
trying to pluck up courage to ask somebody the time. 'Last time
he claimed to have jet-lag,' said my roommate, who now smelt like
a herbal border. 'Wonder what it'll be this time?'

He told us the programme for the weekend. On the Saturday
morning we were to be taken on a bus tour of the Cotswolds. In
the afternoon (and it was a really warm day, remember) we were
to be split into two teams, one of men, the other of women, who
would then play each other at darts. On Sunday there was to be
more darts. At night there would be discos. Oh yes, and we
should be allowed to pick any item from the *á la carte* menu.

The irony was that this little speech broke the ice among the
Singlers. Most grumbled. A few looked at each other with
incredulity. One looked pop-eyed with rage. But Singlers are
gentle people. At dinner we earnestly chose the most expensive
items from a menu crackling with French. *La Galantine á Canard
Truffée. Pintadeau á la Vigneronne.* And one amazing dish which I
translated as being kidneys in their petticoats. We conferred with
each other. We sought each other's advice. We listened, entranced,
as each in turn ordered some meaningless overpriced item. It was
suddenly Singlers versus the rest of the world.

But dinner, after the French and the ordering, was stiff. There
was a lot of shyness. Topics were stumbled on, or frantically
unearthed, only to be buried again: the price of fish; bicycling in
London. But then a girl arrived late and said she had come by
motorcycle. We quivered with excitement. Did she… did she
always travel by motorcycle?

'Yeah. Off North next weekend for a show.'

Was she… was she a dancer? Some of us had stopped breathing.

'Oh no. I play bagpipes. Dagenham Girl Pipers.'

We were talking about her two days later: the Singlers had acquired their first character.

We were wary of each other, and of that sense of failure we knew we shared but none of us would mention. A large confident redhead sat at another table, smoking languidly between courses. I said to my neighbour that I didn't think she could be a Singler, and was asked, sharply, 'Why?' Tread softly, tread softly. After dinner I began to drink, very quietly and deliberately — doubles of white port with Carlsberg Specials as chasers. If man ever gets to the stars it will be on something of this kind.

The next day was our bus tour. The driver had a sense of history hazier than that of mediaeval man: "undreds of years old, that,' he nodded at a castle. A country house showed through the trees. 'Very old, hmmm,' he confided to us. He reserved his fascination for matters of finance. He told us about rate increases in villages, of the cost of housing, of the dilatoriness of farmers with bills. 'Us got summin for everyone, round 'ere. Hospitals for the sick, prisons for bad 'uns, schools for illiterates.' He swung his bus through the lanes like a Panzer commander, awarded us three-quarters of an hour in Bourton on the Water, a genteel tiny Blackpool, half an hour in Stow, and then whisked us home. The Cotswolds were just wallpaper to us Singlers.

We were a group now. There was a dignity to being a Singler. One or two who had met on earlier weekends talked of the Super Singler, a dapper man with an expensive car, who, it was rumoured, came to every weekend. He regarded himself as of too high a rank to talk to most of us, and in public was usually seen with the disappearing host.

On Saturday afternoon we rebelled. Nobody went indoors for the darts match. Instead we lay, white and veined, by the hotel pool and watched the local teenagers basking like little bronze gods. The Super Singler, in some kind of G-string, lay apart from the rest of us. The host was nowhere to be seen.

There was a wedding reception in the hotel that afternoon, and rounding a corner I came on a young married couple quarrelling with that quiet bitterness you only get in marriage. Was it for this we had forked out our cash? But nobody admitted to having come specifically to meet a mate. A young widow said she'd come to get away from the kids, and to be looked after; it also relieved her of the embarrassments of being a woman alone in a hotel. The Dagenham Girl Piper said she'd come because she fancied a week-end in the country. Only one, a woman, after many drinks told me quietly that such a weekend afforded the kindest, most uncompli-cated form of sexual release.

That night at the discos the dancers were closer.

It rained in the night and the next morning, and the thin host who had popped up from somewhere muttered something about a darts championship. Alas, nobody in the hotel could find the darts. We tried bar billiards, but the table machinery had broken. So we played bar pool and, oddly enough, it was the best time of the weekend. We were doing Something, we were not just being Singlers. My roommate, smelling like a large boiled sweet, was Pool King, modestly advising the rabbits on their strokes. Then there was the lady-novice-who-was-good, and the lady-novice-who-was-terrible-but-giggled. Suddenly there was no tension and no awkwardness. Yet after lunch we left the way people do when a ship enters harbour. There were lives to be picked up again, and a few polite farewells. I doubt if many addresses were exchanged.

As an organised weekend, it was something of which the Singles industry should be ashamed. But why should they bother? No industry that trades on human loneliness can ever fail. It was so much easier once when we lived generation after generation in small towns of 12,000 people and knew half of them. Now we turn up in cities like survivors of shipwreck.

The irony is that abruptly it would seem to be much better to be homosexual. They are organised. They have clubs. They have newspapers. The London borough of Islington had even helped finance a homosexual introduction agency, to which went the lesbians, transsexuals, transvestites and homosexuals new to London, on different nights of course. But the poor old heterosexuals had to finance themselves to be allowed to play darts in the Cotswolds. Only, of course, the darts couldn't be found.

The Middle of England

Mixed Emotions

I N THE PUB THE scent was so heavy it was as though I had walked out of an English village and into a tropical rain forest. I looked around me and on every table there were scattered stalks and leaves — so whatever had been there had clearly been gathered up in a rush. Fred Huggins was behind the bar, staring into space.

On 31 August 1997 Diana, Princess of Wales, died in a car crash, and a week later was buried at Althorp, her family home in Northamptonshire. At some point between these two dates Di Huggins of Abthorp, also in Northamptonshire, fell into a rabbit hole and broke her ankle. Mrs Huggins, the wife of Fred Huggins, licensee of the New Inn, had been out looking for a lost cat in the dark.

It was two days later, just after 12.00 noon, a quiet time with the pub not long open, and Mr Huggins was doing the *Telegraph* crossword. He looked up when the door opened to see a man standing there.

'I've got some flowers for Di in the van,' said the man.

'That's very nice,' said Fred.

'Where do I take them?'

'You can bring them in here, put them on that table.'

Mr Huggins returned to his crossword. An addict, he once found a crossword, untouched, in a five-year-old copy of the *Sunday Express* someone had left in a farmhouse in the Falklands. Sergeant-Major Huggins, then in the middle of a war, completed it, and when the war was over he sent the crossword to the paper, apologising for the fact that it was a bit late. His letter was printed, and for a while Mr Huggins, to his amazement, found he was having more mail than the entire battalion. Among those who wrote was the lady who became his wife.

Now anyone capable of completing a crossword with shells bursting overhead is not a man easily deflected. But on that day in August the smell of massed flowers began to register, and when Fred looked up there were tables covered with them. And the delivery man was still coming and going.

'Good God,' said Fred, 'who sent all these?'

'People, mate, just ordinary people. Just shows what they think of her.'

'I didn't realise Di was that popular.'

For a moment the man stared, his eyes bulging.

'Well, you're the only man in England then.'

'But it was all so unnecessary. I mean, what was she doing out there at that time of night?'

'Live and let live, mate. She'd been through a lot, she had.'

'What do you mean?'

But the door had slammed, and to Fred's amazement even the skittle table had disappeared under a covering of flowers. The cats, unable to find anywhere to lie, were prowling irritably. Then the delivery man was back again, his arms full of roses.

'If you don't mind my asking,' said Fred, 'are there any more?'

'Almost done, mate. Just some big lilies, and that's it. Hey, you couldn't run to a cup of coffee, could you? It took me an hour to find this place.'

They sat at the bar together, two men among flowers, like gods of the old world. Flowers unopened, flowers in full bloom, some brought halfway across the world by jet, some from the most expensive glasshouses in England. The seasons and the turning globe had all been stopped to allow this crop of tulips and carnations, roses and lilies. And the smell... a man could reach out and roll it in his hands.

'Lovely flowers for a lovely lady.'

'They are, aren't they.'

'I saw her once, you know.'

'You saw Di?'

'Yes, in Northampton, this was...'

'At the Cash and Carry?'

'Come on, this was in the street, she was going by in a car.'

'Really?'

'God, she was lovely. I'd give anything to see her now.

'But you can. She's on her feet again, now. She'll be down in a minute. What's the matter? Oh my God, you...'

In a pub in Middle England two men stared at each other. Neither was breathing. When I came in there was just the one, who, when he moved, moved like a man in water.

A Man Who Fell
to Earth

THIS IS THE story of a fall.

From morn to noon he fell, from noon to dewy eve.
A summer's day; and with the setting sun
Dropped from the zenith like a falling star...

Well, it must have seemed like that, for afterwards he did not talk about it much, and those people he told muttered asides about the ravings of old men. At least, they did at first, when even his own daughter did not believe him. He was 80 when he fell 45 feet from the church roof. He lay thoughtfully in the earth for quite some time, then got up and walked the mile home to his tea.

I, too, was on my way home, having failed to get an answer at the house where the key to the church was kept, but then through the trees I saw a light in the nave windows. A man with a line of primed mousetraps in front of him was pushing them under the organ. Not exactly Christian behaviour, he said, but it was either that or no music. And these mice were so fat, not like church mice at all. He was in his seventies, neatly dressed, the sort of man on whom all churches now depend, in energetic retirement turning his hands to most things. Honourable men. Guardians.

As we walked along the aisle, his vendetta postponed, he walked about the church as though it were an elderly relative, pointing to the small Norman tiles so casually hacked into by parsons to make way for their own tombs. Above the pillars were unnervingly real stone heads left by the Knight Hospitallers. The centuries were moving like windscreen wipers as he laid his hand on a rood screen to which Cromwell's men had tethered their horses.

The church safe was stolen in my guide's time, only to be found years later after a drought at the bottom of a pond, everything written in the old ledgers still legible. But all the entries in modern ink had gone, the record of his own marriage amongst them. Helpfully he informed the makers of Quink of this, but the makers of Quink seemed not to share his interest.

And then he told me of the Fall. Another guardian, his father-in-law, had taken a stepladder up so he might climb from the chancel to the nave roof. But it was wet and the ladder slipped. 'Now if he'd landed a few feet to his right or a few feet to his left, he'd have been dead, but he landed on the one spot where there was no building and no gravestones. If it had been a dry summer or a cold winter, that would have been the end. But the weather was mild, there had been a lot of rain and the earth was soft. When my wife, a schoolteacher, got home, her father did not have a cup of tea ready as he usually did. She noticed he was very pale and was not saying much. So she made the tea herself, they sat down, and after a while he told her. She felt very sad, thinking her father had begun to go a bit funny.

'But after tea she went down to the graveyard with a flashlight and saw the steps fallen at the side of the church. Beside them was this strange shape in the ground. When she shone the light on it she said it was the perfect outline of a man, inches deep. The arms were wide and the shape of the fingers was there, the legs, everything. She took her father to the doctor that night. He examined him, found nothing at all wrong and taking her aside began to talk about hardening arteries. He said it was sad but there it was, she would have to live with such tales.

'And then she told him what she'd seen.'

The old gentleman lived on for fifteen years, dying at 95. In another age the faces on the pillars would have been round him in a half circle, accusing him of trying to fly. But Harold Crump chose the right century when he fell off the roof of Harrington Church near Market Harborough.

The Riddle of
Brixworth

I T WILL NOT BE headline news, there will be no ITN reporter breathlessly repeating his 200 bald words to camera: all that will happen is that later this year a laboratory report will come through the post. But this could be the answer to one of the oldest riddles in British archaeology as men may finally know the true age of Brixworth Church.

The Reverend Anthony Watkins has been Vicar of Brixworth in the county of Northampton for just a year. He came after ten years in two of the oldest buildings in the country, Chester Cathedral and Tewkesbury Abbey; but nothing he saw in either prepared him for his new church. 'I remember getting off the bus, and then I saw it. I get the same feeling now, especially late at night. It's an uncomfortable feeling. There's nothing scary about it. The place just isn't anyone's idea of a parish church: it feels like something much more, there's something tangible there. You are looking at a church, and yet at the same time there's something quite unreal about it.'

When you come by car from Northampton you see it first

rising up among the bungalows at the start of Brixworth like any conventional church with its spire. Later, from the older ironstone village at its foot, you are conscious only of its size, on the ridge among the winds.

As in most Midlands villages, there is a counterpoint, a Methodist chapel, a brick building put in in 1811, now in ruins; but the life and death of Nonconformity was a mere half-hour in its history. There is the stump of a village cross, so old the stone is blurred; and the church was centuries old when that was new.

No, the real shock comes when you first step inside, and you are in a building the like of which you have never seen anywhere in these islands. Not Norman, no cascades of carved stone and pride. Not even any Saxon style you have ever seen, there is no homely weight here. There is just austerity and elegance and great height. You are in a rectangular hall ending in a raised half circle at the altar, and there are high arches and a triple window looking down on the nave. A suspicion comes that you are in an alien place.

You remember a sentence you once read: 'In the cold fogs of Scandinavia and beside icy Russian rivers, in Venetian counting houses or Western castles, in Christian France and Italy as well as in the Mussulman East, all through the ages folk dreamed of Byzantium, the incomparable city, radiant in a blaze of gold.' In the middle of England you are in a place which seems to reach out beyond our native history to the certainties of a greater civilisation.

Nothing led away from this, no other church in Britain has survived on this scale in this style. The Church of All Saints at Brixworth could have materialised upon its ridge as abruptly as the cabinet of Dr Who.

George Freeston, antiquary and local historian, has known Brixworth all his life. 'It feels so odd, all that great space. The English church started off as a small structure, and then men built outwards and added side aisles. But here there just seems to have been an explosion at the start. That vast zeppelin hangar seems to have been there in the first instance. It's quite incredible'.

Consider one fact. Between 1832 and 1873 the Vicar of Brixworth was the Reverend Charles Watkins, a remarkable man. The Reverend Watkins took out all the mediaeval stained glass in his church. Just think for a moment how you would react if you heard about that now. But the archaeologists working in the church venerate the vicar's memory, for mediaeval stained glass is as appropriate in Brixworth as plywood would be in a castle. He took out the windows to restore the great arches they obscured.

He did much more. He demolished the mediaeval squareended chancel, for he found it concealed something very mysterious indeed. In the course of burying his parishioners he had come on the remains of an apse and, beneath that, a passage crypt around which the faithful had processed.

Watkins was the first incumbent to address himself to the riddle of Brixworth, and has not been the last. Almost without exception his successors have peered into graves and all the building works necessary for repair, while wild theories have passed through their minds. Why had the great 15-foot door, now filled in, been built at the west end? For what ritual, what great man? Names loomed up. For whom had the room in the tower behind the triple windows been constructed? Was it Offa, King of Mercia, who considered himself the equal of the Emperor Charlemagne?

Where had the stones come from? In an area rich in ironstone, geologists have identified 40 different kinds of stone in Brixworth

Church. Why had men gone to such trouble? It has been reckoned that the cost of carting stone in the Middle Ages was just as expensive as quarrying it. And what does the small stone reliquary which was found in the wall of the south aisle in 1809 contain? On being opened this was seen to have in it, 'a fragment of bone and a scrap of filament of Paper or Parchment, which had the appearance of a cobweb, and on opening the box, fell to pieces', recorded the parish register. Had that been the reason for the passage crypt, the holy relic around which the procession moved? What saint, what terrible martyrdom in the forests, did that commemorate? Had that alone been the reason for the grandeur?

Or was this something far more mysterious? Around the arches were Roman tiles, and the church itself was a perfect basilica, the court of justice of the Roman Empire, borrowed, as was so much else, by the early Christians, and the oldest of which, dating from the fifth century, still survives in Ravenna. There was the long rectangular hall. There was the apse where the judge would have sat. What was all this doing in a Midlands village?

So what if it was already there when the missionaries came to pagan Mercia? Could this building have been — as a Saxon poet wrote of a ruin so incredible he could think of no other origin for it — the work of giants? What if out of the twilight of Roman Britain just one building survived, not as a ruin but adapted and maintained so that it was still there, and in use, a millenium and a half later?

There was so little to go on. There was the statement of Hugo Candidus, a monk of Peterborough, writing in the twelfth century, that Brixworth was one of the daughter houses of Peterborough. He implied that as such its date would be late seventh century: even perhaps, as the guide books now claim, around AD68. If that is true, then this is the oldest complete church in Britain. It is certainly the grandest. One architectural historian had no doubts. Brixworth, wrote Sir Alfred Clapham in 1930, was the most imposing architectural memorial surviving north of the Alps in the seventh century. But why was it so grand?

Horace Phillips has been a parishioner here since the fifties, a retired lecturer who occasionally acts as a guide for the curious. His tours, as he admits, consist of questions to which the only answers would be conjecture. Mr Phillips does not conjecture. 'Why was it here? Why was it so prominent so that it could be seen from all horizons?' Like jesting Pilate, he does not stay for an answer. 'All we know,' murmured Mr Phillips, 'is that we are driven further and further back by the evidence.'

Whenever a new heating system was installed or new drainage works carried out, questions like these formed in the minds of men staring into the turned earth. There were no answers, for the open-cast iron ore diggings of the late nineteenth century destroyed the archaeological evidence around the church.

But for the last ten years a committee under the chairmanship of Rosemary Cramp, Professor of Saxon Archaeology at Durham, has been conducting a co-ordinated programme of research. Whenever a bit of plaster came off the walls they descended on it like crows, brooded a parishioner. When a new vicarage was built ten years ago they dug trenches; but as far as the church itself was concerned, they had to content themselves with a stone-by-stone survey.

Until last year. Then when a new drainage system was installed, they dug for the first time in the foundations of the church itself. The dating of what they have found may determine the age of Brixworth once and for all.

David Parsons, Senior Lecturer in Adult Education at the University of Leicester, is co-ordinator of research for the project. He summarised what has been discovered so far. The survey of the walls has led to an identification of 40 different types of stone. There is brick and, even, granite, and Mr Parsons is inclined to believe that some ancient building was plundered. The Jewry Wall in Leicester, as he points out, one of the few bits of Roman wall left standing, looks very much like the side wall at Brixworth.

'But where the building was that was plundered is one of the problems we have to solve. I know it looks like a basilica, but that could partly be the common inheritance of Rome and partly the use of Roman building materials. But we would need a context for it actually to be a Roman building. What was such a great palatial hall doing here? If it had to do with the administration of justice, then why was it here? If you could find a Roman town, yes. What worries us is the lack of context.'

The excavation of the old vicarage showed evidence of a ditch in which burials had occurred. Radio carbon dating of bone indicated a date in the late seventh or eighth century, so it was possible that they had stumbled on the edge of an Anglo-Saxon monastic cemetery. But another dating, this time of what was believed to be the remains of a scaffolding pole high in the south wall of the church, was more startling. This, at the level of the clerestory, was found to be ninth century.

Now before this nobody had doubted that the windows high in the nave were part of the original foundation. If this was so, then the church could not be seventh century. But there were other indications, like the remains of the great triple arcade which the Reverend Charles Watkins found separating nave and choir, which had only been found in the seventh century in this country. So Parsons was forced back on the theory that the clerestory was not initially there.

He now envisages a strange building in terms of what we have come to regard as a church, which had no tower but ended in a large porch or narthex at the west end. In the nave there were a series of arcades leading into what might have been small side chapels. The present dig has allowed access to the foundations of these for the first time, and it is on the dating of materials found there that the future history of the church could turn.

Mr Parsons suspects a ninth century foundation, though he is hedging his bets, for such a dating would really upset the apple-cart. And even a series of consistent dates will not unravel some of the riddles. There is the grand staircase leading to the room above the nave. That, as Mr Parsons says, argues for some great patron. Could it have been a Mercian king? Brixworth is in the heartland of Mercia. In the late seventh century Weedon Bec, some 5 miles away, was the seat of Wulphere, the Mercian King, and the royal family had a deeply religious strain; two of Wulphere's successors resigned to become monks. Saxon royalty did not do that when the going was good.

There is also some tradition of a royal connection, for the church was still in the King's hands at Domesday. So could that great patron have been the greatest Mercian king of all, the late eighth-century Offa? Mr Parsons dreams of finding some kind of palace nearby, which could bear out another traditional belief, that the relic found is the larynx bone of St Boniface, the eighth-century English missionary to the Germans, who murdered him in AD754. It is known that another relic of St Boniface was given to Westminster in the late eighth century. The donor was Offa of Mercia.

It would all make sense if some connection could be found. The irony is that at the centre of all the speculation is an English parish church, not a cathedral; not a ruin, but a working parish church. It is not on the tourist routes and the coaches do not call.

Its congregation, for the most part, remains oblivious to the comings and goings of archaeologists, and there are no elaborate tombs to bring the brass rubbers. There is not even an organ; just a piano through which a piece of the roof once fell.

But then it needs none of these things. The South Door is Norman, twelfth-century, and anywhere else would be one of the most remarkable features of a church, indexed reverently in the guidebook. Not here. Above this door, walled up and shadowy, are the remains of a much taller arch, much older, much grander. There is a side chapel built by a fourteenth-century lord of the manor. 'Simon Curteis who built this aisle lies here; he also greatly embellished this chapel ... Whoso will pray for his soul shall have 140 days pardon.' He needs your prayers for the sheer cheek of what he had caused to be built.

For this is the old, old place.

Last of England's
Village Voices

A VILLAGE IN ENGLAND is a strange place now. The old families, their names in the churchyard and on the war memorial, are leaving. There is no work for them on the land and nowhere they can afford to live; and the young commuting professionals have come, to unbrick a few inglenooks and move on. So, suddenly, this is a place without continuity, and when that goes, folklore and a known past follow; the village becomes thin as a film set, mysterious as a railway terminus. All you can hope for is that, as in the Dark Ages, someone will see to it that something endures.

Such men have always existed. Three hundred years ago there was John Aubrey salvaging manuscripts and memories, anything which would allow men to see the footprints leading up to them. 'These remains are like fragments of a shipwreck that, after the revolution of so many years and governments, have escaped the teeth of time and (which is more dangerous) the teeth of mistaken zeal.' In our time there is Mr George Freeston of Blisworth in Northamptonshire, 90 years old this year. He was born in the

village and has left it only once: when the government invited him
to make war on Germany. He used to be the taxi driver, his father
the undertaker, so nothing moved in Blisworth, or stopped
moving, without their knowledge.

George has recorded everything: its squires, parsons, ghosts,
schoolmasters, adulterers; its changing jobs (of 2,000 people, perhaps 20 now work on the land); the closing of the station, the
coming of the by-pass and of strangers to the housing estate.
Even a man whose photograph he unearths with the pride of a
millionaire showing off his Monet. 'He was the last around here
to be employed to bit lambs' tails off.' One room in his cottage is
filled from floor to ceiling with boxes marked 'Canal', 'Parsons',
'Home Guard'.

Someone said of John Aubrey that he would break his neck in
his enthusiasm for new facts. When navvies, in the interest of
tourism, virtually rebuilt the canal tunnel under Blisworth Hill,
George, then in his middle seventies, splashed through the mud
after them, photographed their machinery, counted the pints they
drank at night, and noted the arrival in suspenders of a kissogram
grandmother from Milton Keynes. When the by-pass came,
George, then nearing 80, was up all night to watch a sectioned
bridge being assembled.

Like Aubrey again, he has found little time for authorship; 'I
now set down things as if they tumbled out of a sack. They will
be of some use to such as love antiquities and natural history.'
George has the same rueful attitude. 'I ought to have written it
down long ago. It should be written down, though I'd need three
secretaries, a housekeeper, and another 50 years. But it'll all be here
for people to find.' When he held an exhibition of local history in
the church, there were television crews and coach tours, and so
many signatures in the visits' book that a new volume had to be

started. Yet everything for the exhibition came out of the one small cottage. 'I can see he's got it all out,' said an old lady, 'What worries me is how he's going to get it all back in again.

It cannot help but have its comic side. When a man lavishes as much attention on a village as a college of arms would on an imperial house, the village sees itself in a new light. They do not throw things away in Blisworth now; they bring George the stuffed owls their grandfathers shot, their old wedding photographs and wills. Last week a man brought his 1966 MOT certificate. 'I think it's time you had this,' he said, handling it as though it were Magna Carta.

History has called on Blisworth. There was Domesday, when the commissioners found a mill (which survived in various forms until 1921); there was Bosworth, when the squire chose the wrong side. The canal tunnel was the most important piece of civil engineering in the early nineteenth century, linking the canals of North and South, so that the Industrial Revolution floated through the village. Its canal port was the busiest in the Midlands, its railway station the crossroads of the region, and they even found iron ore there in 1852. Blisworth should have become an important town, but it all passed by; all of it.

The village is just a line of old houses along two roads now; that and the new estate which has doubled the population. There is just one local employer, the abbatoir down the Northampton Road with a staff of 200. And to residents and motorists the village would just be somewhere on the way to somewhere else were it not for one thing: Mr George Freeston lives in Blisworth.

The novelist J.L. Carr introduced me to George ten years ago, remarking that I should never again need to invent anything for the newspapers. There were two houses worth seeing in the county, he said. One was the Duke of Buccleuch's Boughton, the other was George Freeston's cottage. On balance, he found George Freeston's the more fascinating.

It used to be three cottages, each with one room up and one down, the upstairs reached by a trapdoor through which George once fell. Because of the rising tide of objects, which meant that on occasion he could not find his bed, he has been obliged to move into the loft, installing stairs he built himself, with a balustrade made out of an old coffin bier. In time, all things get used. You come to the house through a garden, past sheep's skulls and old tombstones, bronze busts of Gladstone and Disraeli, fossils and moletraps, a slate cattle trough, and a 6-foot thermometer which used to stand outside the last village butcher's shop.

George has kept notes on the old butcher's reactions to his first wireless set. 'Mine says it's going to rain, what does yours say?' The butcher became an enthusiastic relayer of the national news. 'This financier, know what he did? He stepped out of an airyplane over the Channel and drowned hisself. And know what he had with him in the plane? He had two shorthorn typists.' George has kept everything.

In the tiny art gallery that is his porch, there are oil paintings of the last train to stop at Blisworth; of the village before the trains, before the car, in snow, in evening sunlight; a military chest belonging to a squire who broke his neck out hunting; a tiller from one of the last commercial narrowboats; a 3-foot pair of tweezers that turns out to have been used to pull up thistles.

'Crikey, you don't half like ornaments,' said a new milkman on his first day. 'Ornaments,' grumbled George Freeston. His whole family, he said, had always treasured things. Canal boat teapots. Brass bottle-jacks for roasting. Pewter pipettes for tasting beer. A camel's bladder, stiffened with lacquer and used as a lightshade until too many children asked to see Mr Freeston's bladder.

Some he rescued. Some he bought. And some he quietly acquired. As a corporal in the RAF, George scuttled across Europe behind the armies, acquiring fifteenth-century bronzes and cherubs from bombed chateaux, which he left in empty shell-boxes beside the road, all addressed to 'George Freeston, Blisworth, Northamptonshire.'

And when he got back from the war, there they all were, some-one having assumed they were his last remains. George was always lucky. The corner cupboard in his dining room had been an apart-ment block for a pig and some hens; and one piece of early nine-teenth-century pottery was being sold as modern fairground rubbish when he came upon it. A lifetime's triumphs among country-house sales, demolition sites, 30 years of crossing and recrossing England in a taxi ('That pottery lion I got when I was taking my nephews and nieces to Whipsnade; I had to take all their money.') When George bought the three cottages with his wartime gratuity of £76, he surfed in on a tidal wave of posses-sions.

Like Aubrey, he has not married. 'People ask me what I've done with my life. I reply, "Nothing, I've just lived here."' He has been church secretary for the past 50 years, keeping the minutes and interpolating whatever bits of local information he thinks rele-vant. Thus, when the roads were bad, he noted how many villagers fell over on the way to church, adding that the vicar's prayer that day had been, 'that by reason of the frailty of our nature we cannot always stand upright'. Had things been different, had his family been able to afford further education, he would probably be an emeritus professor elsewhere. As it is, he has no ambition to specialise. 'With me it's people, past and present. You can't talk to an academic historian about anything outside his subject.'

When the canal was nationalised he found its records abandoned in the rain; he has the letters of protest and apology; details of illnesses ('Regret have fallen on head'), and wages, all its social detail. In diocesan records he came across the history of the village school: thus a remarkable man staggers to his feet, a seventeenth-century schoolmaster accused of drunkenness, in particular for his claim that over six nights, armed only with a fork, he fought the Devil; the authorities dismissed him, ignoring the grandeur of his defence that the fight had been a draw.

George has recorded the oral memories of the old who could remember the last dancing bear. And once, asking whether anyone knew anything of the time that the trade unionist Joseph Arch had come, he was stunned when an old man said he did not remember that, but his mother had told him Joan of Arc had come to Blisworth.

When anyone wants to know anything about the village, it is to him they write. Eight years ago, a letter came from Florida, from a man named Stone who had found reference in the library of Congress to a Hussar officer of that name, and to a Blisworth connection. George had grown up seeing that name on graves dug when the Stones were the village squires. One by one he traced them to the royal library at Windsor and Gwent county council ('The Stones got everywhere').

It has been an extraordinary eight years of letters in George's exquisite calligraphy going weekly across the Atlantic. Then one summer the American came to meet his unpaid genealogist, and it was something of an anti-climax. 'He was the sort of man who could go out of my life next week and I wouldn't want to see him again. But I've loved the quest.' George Freeston is a happy man. 'I think this village will survive,' he said. 'And, it'll even survive in a form which we would recognise. The old people, they would never have complained about anything; but these, they'll organise petitions. I think that is one of the biggest changes. The man who moved in yesterday, he'll see to it that Blisworth survives.'

An academic historian would ask, what has the man written? There is the amazing scrapbook, 3 feet by 2, which he submitted in Coronation Year for a competition on local history; a march-past of Blisworth's parsons, brides and bargees, illustrated by his own watercolours. Apart from that he has written nothing.

But from lectures delivered without notes in a hundred schools and church halls, and from the way he responds to people who turn up at his door ('Ah, then you must be the great grandson of so and so'), he has aroused more enthusiasm for the past than any academic historian. When I think of him, I am reminded of R.S. Thomas's lines on the country clergy:

> They left no books
> Memorial to their lonely thought
> In grey parishes; rather they wrote
> On men's hearts and in the minds
> Of young children...

A happy birthday, George. I doubt whether I shall meet anyone like you again.

England and a Wake

IT WAS STRAIGHT out of *Kind Hearts and Coronets*, and all that was missing was Alec Guinness. The generations of admirals and generals, of vicars and colonial magistrates, had so filled the church that the family in this century took to recording its deaths in a book; they keep this in a locked glass case. "Straordinary how few people know their eight great-grandparents,' brooded the 14th baronet. He would not have been able to avoid his had he tried. At home they stare down at him from the walls, faces flicking back into lace and shadow. In church, when his attention wanders, there they are in marble.

'They used to bury us under the organ,' said Sir Hereward Wake of Courteenhall. 'When that filled up we went into a big hole in the churchyard. I think there's a dozen of us in that, the last of them my great-aunt Lucy. But this is a parish church, we accentuate that strongly. We've only been here 350 years — *this time*.'

This year, for the first time in the history of local government, a county council presented one of its poll-tax payers with his family history. Not a pamphlet. The Wakes of Northamptonshire by Professor Peter Gordon (Northants County Council, £19.50) is the size of a family Bible and a thing of beauty. Yet it is still nothing more nor less than an account of a single family. Only there happen to be 29 generations of this family, without break or illegitimacy, or even descent in the female line. The one surname is carried like a horse's skull through the centuries, tweeds giving way to brocade to slashed velvet to ironmongery. 'We started in Normandy...' writes Sir Hereward in his preface, like a man with a bus timetable.

An old family... There is of course no such thing, for all families are old, otherwise none of us would be here, and, as the 14th Earl of Home pointed out in his one recorded joke, even Harold Wilson had to be the 14th Mr Wilson. But it mattered... God, how it mattered once. 'What is an old family but ancient money?' sniffed Lord Burghley, Elizabeth I's minister, but then, as a first generation grandee, he would have had trouble with his full complement of great grandparents. Sir John Wynn of Gwydir, sixteenth-century Welsh squire and rogue, would have had no trouble with his, or with anyone else's. 'A great temporal blessing it is, and a great heart's ease to a man, to find himself well descended,' purred Sir John, quietly grafting a few more princes on to his family tree.

What lies they told, those hard-faced men who had done well out of monasteries or sheep or army catering, and if they lacked the imagination, the quick-witted genealogist could accommodate them. But what if there were a family with no need to lie, a family with the generations stitched into the centuries and not a banker or a brewer in sight, just the unbroken line going back to the Norman knight? David Williamson of Debrett's says that at most there are only six families in our old class-conscious England. What is it like to belong to one and never have had anything to prove? 'Nothing special about us,' said Sir Hereward Wake. 'It's just that we have records.'

Alas, they have felt obliged to go back even beyond these. We were standing in the churchyard at Courteenhall looking at the graves of his grandfather Sir Herewald, the 12th baronet, and of his aunt Thurfride. Up until then the Wakes had names like Charles or Hugh or Baldwin. 'Then the family read Charles Kingsley,' said Sir Hereward.

The first known Wake is Geoffrey Wac, an eleventh-century Norman knight, who must be spinning like a top in his unknown grave at the news that his descendants now claim as an ancestor someone he would have remembered as a Saxon terrorist. But then Sir Geoffrey had not read Charles Kingsley's novel *Hereward the Wake*.

The claim is not entirely batty, for Geoffrey did marry an heiress of Bourne in Lincolnshire, and an historical Hereward is known to have held land in Bourne. But a nineteenth-century professor of Anglo-Saxon at Oxford thought it was, and said as much in a letter to Sir Herewald. 'The whole of this story is highly suspicious...'. Undeterred, Sir Herewald went on christening his children with names he had found in the *Anglo-Saxon Chronicle*, and wrote back to say that the Wakes all had distinct Saxon features: 'light coloured hair and eyes, and *nez retroussé*.' The present baronet, with light-coloured hair and eyes and *nez retroussé*, was nicknamed Toby until he inherited, when he became Sir Hereward, like his own father. They are a dogged family. This is a story about hanging on.

The Wakes appeared in Northamptonshire in 1265, when they inherited Blisworth just down the road from Courteenhall. From here they rode out to fight the Welsh and the Scots, died in French sieges and on Crusades: most of them died young. But the carts creaked up Watling Street bringing new heiresses and they hung on until Bosworth when they fought on the wrong side. The

Wakes, as usual, were for their King. Sir Hereward has just had the tomb restored in Blisworth Church of Sir Roger, the man who made that mistake. 'A man shouldn't let the tomb of his great-great-great... whatever it is... grandfather look a disgrace,' he said.

It is not the oldest Wake tombstone. That turned up in Stamford in 1969 when a house was being demolished, and had been used at some time for building material. This was to a Lady Wake who died in 1380 in the heady days when, his grandmother a Wake, cousin Richard was King of England. The relationship was not close enough for him to drag the family down with him at his fall. 'Stamford were kind enough to give me a copy of the stone, only I didn't know what to do with it...'. Not surprising, considering how the family has filled Courteenhall Church. 'In the end I put it in the belfry.'

After Bosworth, the family sold up and went walkabout. There was a fortunate marriage which set them up in Somerset and allowed them to buy one of James I's new-fangled baronetcies. But oh calamity, as the actor Robertson Hare used to say, there were the Civil Wars: the Wakes rode out to fight for their King and lost the lot in one of Cromwell's gaols.

William Wake, a later Archbishop of Canterbury, wrote movingly to his son, 'Tho' it has pleased God to reduce us to a very moderate Fortune yet somewhat there will occur ... to inspire us with a desire of reviving us again the honour of a name that once was so great in the annals of our country...'. And the 'somewhat' did indeed turn up. His name was Sam Jones. Today he kneels in alabaster in Courteenhall Church, one of only three tombs not to a Wake. Sir Hereward has also had this tomb restored, but then, as I suggested, he has a lot to be grateful to Jones for. 'Indeed,' said Sir Hereward with feeling.

Sam Jones was a London merchant, and a rich one. 'The trouble with us Wakes is that we never had money, we were never in commerce,' grumbled Sir Hereward. During the Civil Wars, Sam was a Parliamentarian, and picked up Courteenhall at a bargain price. The King came into his own again, and Sam turned Royalist; unlike the Wakes, he knew the right side. He was a landed gentleman now and interested in other men's family trees, even those of ruined baronets. His great-niece married the second baronet's son, and inching its way slowly across the family, Courteenhall came to the sixth baronet who promptly changed his name to Wake-Jones. But the seventh had no such scruples, so the name Jones was sent spinning away, like a piece of discarded space technology.

No wars now, these were years when the Park was landscaped and the house built which now stands there. No travels either. Richard Wake, who as the second son is vicar of Courteenhall, comes running across the Park to assure his brother Sir William, on his death-bed, that he is going to Heaven. 'I don't want to go to Heaven,' said old Sir William. 'Courteenhall's good enough for me.' The railway came, cutting through their estate, and they objected to that, just as they would object to the motorcar which would bring the M1 through the estate. But what interrupted the idyll was the fertility of the family. The 10th baronet had twelve children, so the Wakes were off to the wars again.

'You can find out a lot about the British Empire just by reading the wall above our old family pew,' said the 14th baronet. 'Not that I was interested in such things when I was a boy. I kept getting stuck on the inscription to Emily, aged sixteen. "She leant upon the cross and died...". Never could work that out, I used to read it over and over.'

Yet just beyond this is Drury's Ride. Sent with despatches from

Constantinople on the eve of the Crimean War, Drury Wake rode across the Balkans in six days and seven nights and permanently damaged his spine. Then there is Herwald's siege (their variations on a name were endless). Holed up in a bungalow during the Indian Mutiny this amazing man actually kept a diary, 'written with the stump of a pencil, on the wall, at any moment that could be snatched, in case we should be scragged...'. Philip, a mounted policeman, rode into the riots of the Australian Gold Rush but cheerfully wrote home. 'The heat is fearful and being very fat, it tells on me...'. As they become recognisable personalities, the Wakes emerge as very human people.

Baldwin, a bad sleeper, was in the habit of drinking his hair shampoo, which contained chloroform. Only one night he drank too much and, peacefully blowing bubbles, Baldwin passed into what the old Welsh chroniclers called the long sleep. But the brother who gave the family most cause for alarm was William, the heir. A century and a half on, the 11th baronet still causes alarm, for this was the man who could have lost the lot. 'The 11th was no damned good, he made a complete hash of things,' said the 14th. 'Luckily he died young.'

William married the daughter of a man who kept a hotel. His father got a doctor's certificate ('Mr Wake is now labouring under a state of *delirium tremens* combined with imbecility...') but William got his Margaret. In 1847, staying in Jersey, he also got a human skeleton for some reason, was unable to pay for it and got clapped in gaol, from which he made an amazing escape; he ordered a piano then sent it back, having first concealed himself in the packing case. William died on the eve of having every tree in the park cut down for ready cash.

And then there was the 12th, Herewald, he of the retrousse nose and the Saxon ambition. Outwardly a hunting squire ('When you're going to take a fence, throw your heart over and jump after it...') he was also a man who could put up this hand-written notice in his woods, 'If there is any bird-nesting this season at all, the little boys or girls will not be my friends any longer...'. Then the real sanction: they will also not be invited to his parties. He thought scythe blades should be attached to the axles of the hated motor-cars, but when he saw young men marching to the Great War there was no play-acting. 'Cannon fodder,' he was heard to mutter.

His eldest son was part of that by then, who had made the Army his career and was just old enough to have met the antediluvian Duke of Cambridge, Commander-in-Chief of the British Army, who asked, 'They tell me you need brains in the Army now. I never had any. Do you?' 'No sir.' 'I thought not,' said the Duke approvingly. Hereward was actually a bright man whose forecasts on the war impressed Lloyd George. During World War II he got Courteenhall Parish Council to form its own Invasion Committee ('Food and Cooking. Miss T Wake: Fuel. Sir Hereward Wake: Housing and Population. Lady Wake...').

P.G. Wodehouse could have invented that. And he would have been proud of inventing the curious figure astride the motorbike accelerating through the park en route for the dust of someone else's attic. The 13th baronet's sister Joan Wake spent her days rescuing historical documents from the gale of the world and virtually single-handed set up the Northamptonshire Records Society. So what did it matter if, applying face powder, she forgot she was wearing spectacles and powdered these so that she collided with the furniture?

She, too, is straight out of Ealing comedy and would have been played by Margaret Rutherford. When the village water supply failed and no action was taken, she simply telegraphed the

Ministry 'Cholera imminent', and of course there were civil servants leaping out of the hedges. Yet she refused to write the family history, saying it would be too boring. 'She was more interested in other people's families,' said her nephew.

He is at the Hall now, a bit deaf after the war ('Someone asked, shooting accident? I said yes, Germans mainly'), and at 76 more interested in his ancestors than when he day-dreamed in the family pew, trying to understand why a girl should have died from leaning on a cross. The book was his idea, but only as a record of his immediate family. It was just that the Professor found he couldn't stop.

'We Wakes wear our descent like our shoes.' It is an image Sir Hereward has used before. 'We don't like to look at them.' The shoes gleam. 'We're not better than anyone else, it's just that we've always been around. I'm an ordinary human being but people seem to expect a lot of me. "Oh Sir Hereward, will you open this?"' But it does allow him some fun. The story is told that he once came upon a new vicar putting up the hymn numbers in Courteenhall Church. 'No. Mistake there. We never have more than two hymns, one psalm, and I read the lesson.'

'According to Church law...' began the startled cleric.

'The only law here is Wake law.'

The dead are closer now, his grandchild in the churchyard and his sister killed in a point-to-point accident ('It was the darkest day. The whole family was there watching'). We hovered over the book in the locked case. 'That was my father's idea, he said we couldn't go on putting Wakes up all over the church.'

'Do you have the key?'

Sir Hereward, who has the key to everything, did not answer. 'It's given us an opportunity to write a few home truths, that book,' he said. 'Things we couldn't put on a wall.'

'Do you have the key?'

After a while he said, 'Look, I'm worried about you. I've read the things you write...'. He unlocked the case, and there were pages of exquisite calligraphy but no home truths. 'Look at that, my father gets five pages. Can you image five pages on a wall?'

Over tea his wife said, 'Didn't you manage to stuff a sexton into that church once?'

'I believe so,' said Sir Hereward vaguely.

He has had the Leper Window unblocked and proposes to have this inscription cut into the stone, 'Remember the lepers and all outcasts'. It is such a poignant message, I was still thinking of it when I got outside and heard the motorway. The MI, a mile away and screened by trees, is an even band of sound as though some huge creature beyond the park were trying to clear its throat. Northampton also gets closer every year.

Norman St John
Stevas Chooses a Title

As YOU WOULD expect, he chose his new title with care, Lord St John – adding 'of Fawsley'. It must have appealed to the romantic in him, for this is a name out of mediaeval chivalry. But there is something else. Because of his title, the former Mr Norman St John-Stevas now enters English history forever linked to one of its blackest moments.

You find that place-name on road signs in the lanes south of Daventry and on the green footpath markers, but it is only when you follow these that you find there is no Fawsley. There is a lake, yes. And a manor house. And a church. Nothing else. Even a century ago the *Northamptonshire Gazeteer* was puzzled. 'There is no village in this parish; it contains but four houses altogether.'

When I first saw it I thought it one of the most beautiful places on earth – the lake at sunset with the swans upon it; the Tudor mansion with its great oriel window; the medieval church, its door so tiny you stoop to enter, standing in grassland with no road leading to it. But nothing prepares you for what is inside the church, the alabaster and brass of the tombs which occupy two-thirds of it, one of them taking up most of a wall. And all to one family, the Knightleys. They were as proud as the Hapsburgs, these Knightleys, with the 334 armorial quarterings to show their descent. At the edge of the woodland the stone arch shows where their world began, the 700 acres of their park.

And yet there is something odd about it all. For instance, the church is centuries older than the manor house, so Fawsley was there long before that. Also nobody built a church in a field. In a closed little world like this, no grandee would have walked 300 yards across his park to worship in his own family church. But there is one clue. When the sun is at the right angle you can see bumps in the grass near the church — not many, for the lake has covered most of the evidence, but enough to show that there were once buildings here.

You have to go to the records for the rest. At Domesday there was a village at Fawsley, and an old one, for the courts of justice had met at the foot of a great beech tree, 19 feet in diameter, chillingly called Mangrave. In the poll tax of Richard II's reign there were 90 taxpayers, which would have made Fawsley one of the largest villages in the county.

Then in 1415 the Knightleys came; and the Knightleys were sheep farmers, whatever their tombs may proclaim. The evictions began in the late fifteenth century and two generations later there were 2,500 sheep. No village. No people. Nobody knows what became of these, it is too long ago and they would have been illiterate. Most of them would have starved, pathetic bundles of rags blown here and there. It is only the emptiness at Fawsley, and in records elsewhere the odd scribbled note 'where 40 people had their livings, now one man and his shepherd hath all', which point to the tragedy.

He might just as well have styled himself Lord St John of Culloden.

Listening for England

I KNEW HIM EVEN before the studio lights came on. I could make out that bulk of neck and shoulders in the back row as George sat four-square, hands palm down on his thighs, facing the cameras like a statue in the Valley of the Kings.

It had begun a week before, during a television documentary, when some woman new to village life said brightly, 'Of course, the worst thing about living in the country is the inconvenience of bulk buying.' This had stopped George in mid-gin.

Because his wife runs the post office, and he sometimes has to deliver the mail, he has come to know all there is to be known about village life. He talks of dead houses, where once birthday and Christmas cards came, and now no letters ever come, because these are weekend cottages. Then there are the other houses where nothing moves after 7.00 in the morning because the commuters have gone by then. So there are these beautifully painted doors with which he can associate no human face.

George is not opposed to change. It is just that an image is pursuing him, of a summer morning in the village where nothing moves in the main street, no children play, but everything is immaculate, and quite dead. The bulk-buying comment confirmed it all. He phoned the programme and spoke for five bitter minutes and was, of course, invited to a studio discussion.

Out of the shires came George to speak for England.

He drove the 300 miles there and back the same day. Such distances are nothing to a man capable of driving 650 miles in a day when he had forgotten his coat in a Sussex pub. Besides, 'after that thing was over, you couldn't have seen my heels for dust'.

At first he had been fascinated by his thirteen fellow guests. Carefully chosen, as he thought, they would surely represent village life in his time. He scanned their faces to see who his enemies might be. An elderly peer took him on one side. 'I... I... I...'. George waited, thinking some ancestral insight was about to come, 'I... I'm deaf.' Then there was the American businessman who kept looking at his watch and talking about the Shuttle he had to catch. Surely, breathed George, surely he wasn't going back to America that night?

'No Birming-hahm.'

George had so much to say. He wanted to tell them about his worries, the cost of housing which now meant his sons could not live in the village, the planning committees which only allowed developments the old families could never afford, and, with the sale of council houses, the lack of rented accommodation.

And he did start to say it, until the sound man came on to the studio floor muttering that the microphones were acting up. Then there were the other voices, insistent and sharp, other faces which caught the chairman's eye. For this was television where the quick and the very quick burgeon like bindweed.

George opened his mouth many times. He moved forward in

his seat and we who know him jerked upright, but then he had moved back again, his head turned towards the speaker, and there was a dignity about him.

All I can remember now about those 22 minutes is the huge escarpment of one man's silence, as George listened for England.

Heroes

Race Against Time

ONE MORNING IN SUMMER, the London to Newquay express train having slowed because of repairs to the sea wall at Dawlish, passengers were startled to see an old gentleman get to his feet and start reading aloud from a book. The book, he told them, was *Through the Window*. This had been published by the Great Western Railway and described all the railside scenery from London to Penzance, provided the train went slow enough for a man to see it. He had bought his copy, he said, in 1927.

He was asked, was he going to Cornwall on holiday? No, said the old gentleman, he was going to Cornwall to race. They tried to hide their smiles and then someone, more daring than the others, asked, what sort of race might that be? The triathlon, said the old gentleman. At that silence fell like a guillotine, for they had all seen on television the iron men of athletics swimming, cycling and running through the landscape. There was some stealthy semaphoring of eyebrows, but most of the passengers began to stare fixedly through the windows. The old gentleman was still reading aloud from his book.

A few weeks earlier a phone had rung in the Ashby de la Zouch headquarters of the British Triathlon Association. The caller was the organiser of the Fowey Triathlon in Cornwall, in which competitors would be expected to swim over a third of a mile across the estuary at high tide, to cycle 18 miles over a switchback landscape and then to run 7 miles, all this without stopping. The caller was a troubled man.

'I've just had this entry form from a man who gives his age at 80. I take it that's a typing error.'

'Oh no, that's Patrick.'

'What do you mean, "That's Patrick"?'

The generation of schoolboys brought up on the *Wizard* comic would have had no doubts. He would have been Wilson, the mysterious athlete taught by a hermit to slow his heart down to 40 beats a minute, who in the 1896 Olympics came second in the 100 metres, 400 metres, long jump, high jump and the shot; coming second in all these events only because he had been savaged by wild dogs while competing in the marathon.

Patrick Barnes was born in 1915. A chartered accountant for 33 years with British Airways, he took little exercise during his working life but in retirement Mr Barnes turned athlete. At 66 he ran his first marathon, at 69 his first triathlon; last summer, at 80, Mr Barnes completed 14 triathlons.

Wilson of the *Wizard*'s first appearance on an athletics track was startling, for he ran barefoot, dressed only in black combinations. Mr Barnes's materialisation in his first triathlon also stunned officials. While the other competitors leapt on to their stripped-down, high-tech bikes, a single frame of which can cost £3,000, Mr Barnes mounted the Raleigh Popular his father had bought for him in 1925. If this were not enough, the thing had a basket on the front and Barnes, to hide its rust, had painted it emerald green. He called it Beelzebub. 'A photograph of me on Beelzebub appeared in a German magazine,' he said stiffly. 'I do not read German but I knew enough of the language to be able to recognise the word "Greenhorn".'

Then there was the matter of his kit. Triathletes, the women alarmingly, turn out in a state not far short of nudity. Mr Barnes wore an old tropical shirt and shorts to his knees; he also wore gym shoes, which he paused to lace after his swim. 'I know he's only had a wet suit for eighteen months,' said Dave Arlen, chairman of the London region of the BTA. 'Before that, I'd never seen anything like it, he just used to get into the water, whatever its temperature. Now for a man of his age to be competing in triathlons was extraordinary enough, but to be competing under those handicaps, with everybody around him in high-tech gear.... And he was completing the courses.'

Fowey was Mr Barnes's 100th triathlon, but it worried him. This was not because the organiser, Tony Bartlett, had rung to describe in very graphic detail the high tides, the waves and the terrible hills. Mr Barnes was worried about his bike.

While competing in triathlons he keeps his teeth in his saddle-bag. Not only is he the one living triathlete to do this, he is probably the only triathlete to have a saddle-bag at all. Also lights. And mud-guards. For, after an accident in 1994 when he wrote off his car, the bike has been his only means of private transport.

Elaine Shaw, chief executive of the BTA, recalled her first meeting with Mr Barnes at an awards dinner held at the Donnington Thistle Hotel. 'The first thing he said was, "Well, you certainly managed to find an inaccessible place." I didn't understand, because the hotel was near a junction of the motorway. It was only later I realised that he'd come by train and cycled the 12 miles from the station, with his dinner suit in the saddle-bag.'

His present bike, a second-hand Dawes 12-speed, is his third. He calls it Pluto, and still owns its predecessors, Mephistopheles and Beelzebub. What worried him about Fowey was that the organisers guaranteed to look after Pluto only for a certain time after the cycle stage was completed; so he could see himself running the 7 miles to Fowey and then back again to claim it – all this without teeth...

The weekend began badly. He got off the train with Pluto (and his copy of *Through the Window*) only to find he had left his cycling safety helmet on a train disappearing down the line to Newquay. British Rail retrieved that for him. He then walked down to the harbour and saw the water, and the wind on the water. That night Mr Barnes prayed ('though I normally consider it bad form to ask God to do personal favours'), and in the morning laid his address book prominently beside his bed in the guest house, the page open at the telephone number of his next-of-kin. Then Mr Barnes went swimming.

The first thing he found was that he could not do his usual crawl because his legs would not move. Following a prostate operation earlier in the year, he had been prescribed steroids by his doctor; these had puffed up his body so that movement within the wet suit became difficult. He settled for a side stroke and began swallowing water in the waves so that his face, as he recalled, came to feel like salted meat. When he got out he could not stand but then, as an onlooker said, he saw some press photographers and he somehow straightened up. As he changed into his shorts and T-shirt there was great applause. And Mr Barnes went cycling.

To be accurate, there were times when he walked as well, noting at one point the site of the greatest Royalist victory in the Civil War. Elite triathletes, as he has observed, notice only gradients and markers; he feels sorry for them as he notices flowers and trees and history. This has, of course, meant that on occasion he has lost his way or fallen with his bike into a bush or, during a triathlon in South Wales, swum steadily towards the open sea. 'Going out with the tide then?' asked a chap in an inflatable, watching him with interest before pulling him on board (for the first time since Dunkirk, noted Mr Barnes).

But that day in Fowey, as the hills became more abrupt, he noted that he couldn't even walk without stopping for rests. 'As one does when climbing Kilimanjaro,' he mused. Since his retirement Mr Barnes has climbed Kilimanjaro four times. One thing he did not like was the way a St John ambulance, primed by the organisers, kept shadowing him along the route, like Death in a foreign art film. Its officers urged him to give up for it was raining and to put his bike in the back. No, said Mr Barnes, he liked to finish his races.

And then the cycle stage was over and Mr Barnes, having come to an arrangement over its retrieval, went running. The sun had come out, there were blackberries as big as grapes in the hedgerows as Mr Barnes, cursing his missing teeth, jogged on, apologising to every marshal he passed for being two hours behind the man in front of him. But at least this was not the Bath Triathlon, where they have a time limit, or the Leicester one, where the race is stopped at sunset, like social life in Transylvania.

'What staggered us was that he finished,' said Lyn Bartlett, the organiser's wife. 'The chap picking up the race markers may have been treading on his heels, but what was so wonderful was that all the young athletes had decided to wait for him. It would have been so depressing if it had just been him and the time-keeper, and they'd said, "If he can do this, then we'll wait for him." So they did.'

In 1993 he represented Britain in the 75–79 age group in the World's Triathlon in Manchester. 'He got a bigger cheer than Spencer Smith who came first,' said Dave Arlen. 'He couldn't understand it and kept saying, "I've got to get away, I've got a train to catch."'

Fowey River Triathlon, 1995: Winner's time, 107 minutes 51 seconds; Mr Patrick Barnes's time, 324 minutes 54 seconds. Mr Barnes was 57th overall, also last. But there is a curious irony to all this, for Mr Barnes did not really come last. Not then, not ever. 'In triathlons results are normally graded by age groups. This is where I come into my own, for although I am nearly always last in the race, I am always first in my age group. The fact that I may be the only one in my age group is of no consequence. In my career as an athlete I have acquired many prizes.'

There is a house near Osterley Park where the cups and plaques are everywhere, contending for space on mantelpiece and sideboard with photographs of grandchildren. Here Mr Barnes has lived alone among his trophies since the death of his wife five years ago, his only other claim to fame being the fact that he is the one surviving member of the prep school Scout patrol once led by Michael Foot.

Keswick Triathlon, 1st man over 60 ('Looks a bit like a tombstone, that one'); Newquay Triathlon, men over 70; Aylesbury, 1992. Like Wilson of the *Wizard*, Patrick Barnes has rarely lost a race, for the only competition he has faced was when he took up the sport and there was a man three years his senior competing, but he got killed hang-gliding. So what made Patrick run?

The only sport he had done consistently was skating and, though for twelve years secretary of the Royal Skating Club, he was, by his own admission, an elephant on ice ('which is why they made me secretary, to keep me off the rink'). Then, one year away from retirement, Mr Barnes was in Tokyo to do an audit and found the streets blocked off for an event he had never watched before, a marathon. 'And it occurred to me that this was not like skating at all. In skating you have to do the thing properly and artistically. In marathon running all you have to do is finish.'

And so, just as Cromwell pondered on what if a man should take upon himself to be King, so Mr Barnes pondered on what if a man should take upon himself to be a marathon runner. In Osterley Park he started by running 200 yards, then a mile, then 5 miles. It took him a year and a half to get up to the 26 miles ('and 585 yards,' said Mr Barnes with feeling). The only thing was that he had measured Osterley Park himself and it was three miles short, which was disastrous for his first races. But Mrs Barnes, he said, was pleased he had found a hobby.

Mr Barnes ran nineteen marathons, among them five in London and five in New York, also the Marathon to Athens, the course on which the race was based. He ran his last in 1993. One reason was that Alice Billson, two years older, whom he had met in various marathons, managed to beat him. It was not the fact that she could run faster, he said, if anything he was the better runner, but Mrs Billson could walk faster, and the intervals of walking had become longer. Nevertheless, it is gossip among athletes that Mr Barnes abandoned the marathon because he could no longer lace up his shoes.

By then, on Beelzebub, he had taken up the triathlon. He had been recommended to do this by his physiotherapist, who had herself run a marathon and thought he was not doing enough training for that event. He took part in the 1984 London Triathlon and came last, so far behind the other competitors that he was kissed by three beauty queens in the Royal Victoria Docks.

Enter the Great Barnes, Triathlete. Of his 100 races to date, he has completed 89.

Sometimes he is cycling when the other athletes have moved into the last, running, stage. They then have the eerie experience of being overtaken by Mr Barnes on a bike. Sometimes he runs a specially shortened course ('otherwise I'd still be out in the country somewhere when they've all packed up and gone'). None of this has deterred him.

'He's a little bit of a hero,' said Elaine Shaw of the BTA. 'He's slow but he finishes. If he's there, he'll be last, but then he ought to be last. I've seen him at the National Championships swimming in the Thames. It was June but God, it was cold.'

'He's a throwback, a man out of his time,' said Dave Arlen. 'This old-fashioned English gentleman competing in a sport that is so new.'

At Osterley Park the throwback had returned from one of the two aerobics classes he goes to each week. 'I'd rather you didn't say too much about training,' said Mr Barnes. 'I am a very lazy man.' He did not think he would do fourteen triathlons this year, he said, but he would do some. He would also do some the year after, which would bring him to within three years of the Millennial Olympics, when the triathlon will be included for the first time. But one question remains unanswered. Why does Patrick run?

It has brought an old-age pensioner much pain and even more expense; he had his hotel bill paid on only one occasion, he said, at Hull. But, when asked directly, all Mr Barnes does is talk about mountains being there. For a fortnight I had been asking the question in different ways and the answers had all been similar. Except once.

'These things happen,' said Mr Barnes.

Mr Sparry Entertains

MR SPARRY INTRODUCED his friends as though they were the heroes of the ancient world. 'This gentleman is well-informed on things like going up chimney stacks,' said Mr Sparry, and you half expected to hear trumpets. A large man looked up without curiosity from his place by the fire. 'And Paul here' – a man in a muffle nodded – 'Paul is just generally intelligent.' The man in the muffler did not argue, for in the world of Mr Sparry, just as in fairy tales, each friend has his appointed role. 'And should you be lucky…'. Mr Sparry paused, and one long white hand moved in the air, 'you could, you just could, meet a man who bumped into King George VI.'

Most afternoons Mr Sparry's friends crowd into his tiny kitchen to wait for the kettle to boil on the sort of black-leaded range you usually find only in museums. They like tea and they like Mr Sparry who is as strange and amiable a man as ever sidled out of the brain of Mr Charles Dickens. That last sentence shows the effect of Mr Sparry.

He is 50 years old, small and very thin with long pale features. He walks and talks with a sort of silky stateliness so that the world you know is suddenly a long way off. Mr Sparry's courtesy and his English are both out of another time ('My father was a natural singer of harmony, which I much envy'); but then he has chosen to live in another time. By trade he is a second-hand book-seller. There are books piled everywhere on the tables and shelves of what was once the front room of a Victorian terraced house in this Black Country village. A wave redevelopment tore through the terrace, bringing new brick shops, but leaving this one house. It left Mr Sparry, too.

He inherited the house from his parents, who had inherited it from his grandparents, who, having bought the house in 1910, built the lean-to kitchen. He has kept everything as it was in their times. 'We were going to have a bathroom built in the 1950s,' mar-velled Mr Sparry, 'but we never got round to it. Lack of money was the reason then. Now it is simply a lack of interest.'

He lives alone and coal fires are his only source of heat. He has an electric kettle which his friends insist he uses when they call late at night, but there is no electric boiler or cooker, and the lava-tory is outside. The result is that the friends who crowd into this kitchen, most of them men around his own age, find themselves crowding mysteriously into their own childhoods. But it also means that Mr Sparry lives in conditions that would have any landlord pilloried in the popular press.

'It's a terrible way to live,' said the Well-Informed Man on the Inside of Chimney Stacks. The street door had opened and Mr Sparry had wandered off to investigate that curiosity, a customer who had come into his shop. 'I put that coal boiler in for him, found him a wooden cover with the old copper nails in as well; and the wash-basin, got him that. Also the boards for his ceiling. The wind used to blow through his slates before that and you could see the sky. I also got his lavatory to work.'

'Mr Hale,' said Mr Sparry, gliding into the room as though on castors, 'has done that by twisting the old pipes into a modern cistern.' The result is a wild art décor design. 'Did that one afternoon when I was having a cup of tea here,' said the designer. Mr Hale, said Mr Sparry, was the Man Who Had Twisted The Pipes.

Mr Hale had earlier talked about his friend. 'How does he live?' Mr Hale took a long swig of tea. 'On potatoes and vegetables. Doesn't smoke or drink or mess wi' women. Eats one raw onion a day, and you should see him do that.' He pointed to a small hatch in the wall. 'His cat used to come through that until it died last year. Been with him eighteen years.' The cat's basket still hangs on the wall, for nothing gets thrown away here.

Two things underwrite John Sparry's lifestyle. The first is the economics of the second-hand book trade. Each year he sets out to earn just £2,400, enough to keep him alive and out of sight; any more and Mr Sparry would have to pay income tax. 'I started doing radio talks about two years ago and that could have wrecked my scheme, but the danger passed. I shall eventually have to make more money but I am placid about it.' For the moment he has the privacy which only billionaires and the last tramps enjoy. The second thing is his interest in the past. One of his two upstairs rooms is given over to mementoes that he has rescued before the gale of the world could blow them away. He has labelled these neatly in red capitals. MR DUMPHY'S OLD HOLLY LOG. MRS HUDSON'S OLD HAT.

'Mrs Hudson was a very interesting old lady,' said Mr Sparry. 'She had a large goitre on her neck, the result of drinking well water. So I kept her hat.' CYRIL HILL'S RED HANDKER-CHIEF. Hill was the local road-sweeper, when he died Mr Sparry kept his handkerchief. 'So much gets thrown away,' he said, 'and this is our history.' The effect is startling. For a moment you find yourself staring at a folded red handkerchief as though it were something that had belonged to Achilles.

For, just as the larger world of bureaucrats has no place in Mr Sparry's own life, so that of conventional historians has no place here. These are not mementoes of public men, for this is the private world of Mr Sparry of which once anything is a part, it casts a giant shadow: the friends by the fire, the handkerchief an old gentleman left, the log someone threw away. Do you understand what this means? This is a house where, as soon as you enter, you find you have lost the anonymity that the late-20th century and its centralised communications network imposes on you. Because of Mr Sparry you feel you are *someone* here.

'Kettle on?' A large face had come round the door. 'Double-glazing,' muttered Mr Hale from his place by the fire, but Mr Sparry the impresario was waving his long fingers. 'This gentleman knows all there is to be known about double-glazing,' he announced. I asked the newcomer if this was so, for I thought they were pulling my leg. 'Someone has to sell double-glazing,' he said cheerfully, 'before that I was in the fish and chip business.' With great restraint Mr Sparry did not proclaim him the Emperor of Batter.

There are just four rooms to the house, plus the lean-to kitchen. The front room downstairs contains the books, the front room upstairs, the relics. Mr Sparry sleeps in the back bedroom, a fascinating room full of treasures, such as an old *Eagle* and a hand-written 1864 Hebrew and Chaldee commentary to the Bible. A Chaldee commentary? 'A lifetime's work,' said Mr Sparry. Over the bed hang four photographs of King Edward's Stourbridge, the local school he once attended. 'That's me' — a small face is peering round someone else's shoulders as though a pixie had strayed into the group. Mr Sparry is not in any of the other photographs but they hang over his bed as well. A book beguilingly entitled *The Treatment of Trade-Waste Waters and the Prevention of River Pollution* will one day be read, since he is interested in reclamation. He is interested in comedians too, and etymologists, and local industrial slang, and teddy bears; he gives talks on each of these to local societies. He keeps notes in labelled plastic bags.

But it is the back room between kitchen and bookshop that is puzzling, being at odds with the other indices to Mr Sparry. The room is full of drums and xylophones, for Mr Sparry is a jazz musician and part of a group. 'This drum was autographed by Eric Delaney,' he said and stopped, puzzled by the lack of reaction. 'You've not heard of Eric Delaney? That is true, is it? You've not heard of Eric Delaney?' Then you begin to appreciate that behind the tea-drinking heroes there is the shadowy outline of even greater men. But such thoughts were interrupted by the door opening as into the kitchen stepped Mr Ray Ashton, The Man Who Bumped into a King. He groaned as he was persuaded to tell the tale – 'Again?' said Mr Ashton.

During the war Mr Ashton was demonstrating the electrical circuit of a car. What sort of day was it? They were in a tent, said Mr Ashton. The ground was uneven, and the King stumbled. He would have fallen had he not collided with Mr Ashton. What had he said to the King? 'Pardon me.' And what had the King said to Mr Ashton? 'Sorry.'

The Examinee

SOUNDS OF SUMMER: a lawnmower clattering into life, the ragged sound of clapping at a village cricket match, a burst of pop music out of nowhere that you do not wish to hear. But there are other sounds of summer. Close your eyes. Listen. No matter how long ago, 30 years, 50, they are vivid now as ever they were. Silence first, but a silence broken when someone coughs. It is a cough in a large room and it echoes, setting off other sounds. Someone moves his feet. There is a rustle of paper. And then it begins. The metronome of footsteps as a man walks up and down, up and down, between the avenues of desks. Remember now? You are back where you never want to be again, in the examination halls of your youth. You are in the hunting preserve of Mr Terry Tyacke of Trowbridge.

Mr Tyacke sat an A level this summer, and the press and television crews descended on Trowbridge, for it was his 22nd A level, and in Physical Education, for, after 20 years of exams, he is beginning to run out of subjects. English, Maths and Geography, he stalked these long ago, seeking them out where they lurked in their various examination boards. He has sat so many that if he gets PE, he will be forced to set his sights on something nobody ever sat at A level. Mr Tyacke will take Philosophy.

'I've been meaning to have a stab at that for some time, but it'll be real hard going, that one,' said Mr Tyacke among his trophies. To be precise, his trophy. On a handwritten piece of notepaper he has recorded subjects, boards, dates and grades.

It all turns on whether he gets PE. It had been a toss-up whether he would take that or Photography this year. 'But I didn't have a camera so I thought that might be a bit of a draw-back with Photography,' he said with the sort of unanswerable logic that augurs well for Philosophy. Even so, he had not taken into account the practical exam in PE which required him to run the 100 metres in 11 seconds, play in a hockey game and throw the javelin. He thinks he may have clocked 11 seconds for his javelin run-up, but his 100 metres was off all the stop-watches and the examiner forgot to bring an egg timer.

'No. I don't mind you laughing,' said Mr Tyacke generously. 'It's a game to me, but you have to admit, it's a very different sort of game from what most people play.' He became a national figure when, egged on by his twelve-year-old grandson, he entered the *Guinness Book of Records*, every new edition of which now has updated his growing bag of A levels. That was when the press started calling. 'Even the *Sun* rang me up. Gave me a shock that did. I can tell you. Luckily they never rang back, for God knows what they might have dug up about me.'

It all began 23 years ago when Susan, his only child, was sitting her O levels, and to keep her company, as he puts it, Terry, a Royal Navy shipwright for 22 years, and his wife Morwenna also signed up for what he calls 'a bundle of O levels'. It is a lovely phrase: you can see the two of them staggering along under the weight. That was the start for the Great Examinee.

A man who had left school without a single O level had passed fourteen of them when he became aware of an even greater escarpment looming above him, and moved into the foothills of A levels. By now exams had become a way of life for the Tyackes, for when Susan left school to join the Civil Service her parents went on. Every summer there was a new bundle, and when the exams were over they treated themselves to a meal out. Mrs Tyacke died in 1992, but her husband could not abandon the old ways.

'I don't want to go to university. That'd be too big a commit-ment. A levels do me, a nine-month job, sign on in September at the local college and then wait. It's a bit like being pregnant really.'

Every September the young get younger, and he is a little older. For History he did not even bother to sign on at any educational establishment, but studied that himself ('I felt I'd lived the bugger'). As for the other subjects, the local college at Trowbridge has a new wing now. Terry feels he has paid for most of it.

The tiny garden in front of his house is so neat that even before you meet him you appreciate that the man is a perfection-ist. He has three hobbies. One is gardening. Another is to follow the fortunes of Arsenal FC with his grandson. The third is exams. It is the neatness about these that appeals to him ('You pays your money and you get a result'). If there is no result, then his inclina-tion is to turn away, as he did when he failed chemistry at O level, but maths brought out a doggedness in him: he sat and re-sat A level Maths until he got 'the buggers'. And once Terry Tyacke, in June 1987, got an A. This was in Business Studies.

'I remember when we came out, we were talking about the exam papers and all the others were groaning about things we hadn't covered. I didn't say anything for I'd sat Accountancy the year before and I'd covered them in that. Things spill over from one subject to another when you've sat as many exams as I have.' In fact, he knows more about exams than any man living, having sat more of them than any man living, and under more examining boards. Oxford, Cambridge, the Associated Examining Board. He didn't think he had sat London, said Mr Tyacke, but he couldn't be sure.

'I remember Young Sir...'. This is how he refers to his various tutors who, like his classmates, are getting alarmingly younger. 'I remember Young Sir suggesting we switch boards for Accountancy and, of course, we were all up in arms. But then he brought in some past papers and I thought, "Hello, this is for me."' Mr Tyacke got B for Accountancy under the Oxford board. Playing the field, he subsequently sat Land Geography, Sociology, Economics and Geology under Oxford.

He does not do well in everything; no man could. Six of his 'A level' grades are E, eight of them D, but they are passes all the same. 'Never mind the quality, feel the width,' said Mr Tyacke, enlarging on his philosophy of education. 'I gets most of my books at Oxfam. You go down there in June and July, and Oxfam's full of books thrown away by people who never want to sit an exam again.'

I began leafing through the British and European History paper he sat in 1993. 'Why, despite the granting of Catholic Emancipation in 1829, was there still an Irish Question?' Mr Tyacke had ticked that. 'Oh, there's always an Irish Question,' he said vaguely. 'But don't ask me anything about it. I revises at the last minute and when the exam is over I forgets the lot.'

Here you have the professional examinee at his most ruthless, jettisoning knowledge like Sherlock Holmes as soon it has no relevance. For, whatever supporters of the system might argue, exams in the end are not about education. They are about exams. Terry agrees. 'I don't think it's the right system. I can sit and swot and pass an exam, but it doesn't make me clever, just crafty. I watch TV news and I see these kids getting their results and it's terrible, the pressure on them. There's no pressure on me. I can go into an exam and I've got no nerves, it's a game. But you should see them … and what prospects have they got? If they can do a job, what does it matter how many A levels they've got? It's all wrong to put on a job advertisement, "Don't apply unless you've got four O levels."'

Asked whether he had any tips for those taking exams he said he had two. The first was to get hold of as many past papers as possible. The second was to read the questions carefully.

'I remember Sociology. This Young Sir said he was sure a question on divorce would not come up this year, but I had a feeling it might. Yet when I looked at the paper it wasn't there, not in any of the fourteen questions, of which we had to answer four. Then, when we came out this Young Maid...', this is how Terry Tyacke refers to the girls in his class, so it sounds that he and they are part of a Nursery Rhyme, 'she said, "You were right, you were right..."'. Then Terry realised that there *had* been a question about divorce, although they hadn't used the actual word. So, 'Read the questions... I'd been waffling on about trade unions. Blow me, I could have got a C.'

His age has long ceased being an embarrassment, having become a joke. 'I've seen a fair few librarians and a few caretakers off in my mind, I can tell you.' He likes the young and they, sensing that this is one grown-up who knows what they are going through, like him. 'Outside college, you could say I was anti-social, but I have had some good laughs with the other students. Perhaps it's because I'm just a big kid myself, but the young chap next door, he's been at the college, said, "Blimey, Terry, don't you realise you are God to them?"'

But his career may soon be over, PE had been a shock, though not the written exam. 'What is blood pressure. How can it be measured?' At 70 a man knows exactly what blood pressure is and how it can be measured. No, it was the practical, during which he surfaced like the Ghost of Christmas Past. 'We were playing hockey and I tackled one chap who said, "God, who are you and where did you come from?" I hadn't encountered anything like that before. I remember my daughter saying, when I told her I was sitting A level English, 'But you don't read books.' I told her you didn't have to read them for exams, just the beginning, the middle and the bit at the end. But when my grandson heard I was doing PE and had to do all this running and that, he just couldn't stop laughing.'

As I write, a man in Trowbridge is trying to make up his mind. Should he call it a day? Or should he go for one last A level? Somewhere out there, beyond reason and what most call common sense, lies Philosophy, which could blow the fuses in a man's mind…

Come, my friends,
'Tis not too late to seek a newer world.
Push off, and sitting well in order smite
The sounding furrows: for my purpose holds
To sail beyond the sunset…

And soon a new term starts.

Glutton for Punishment

I HAD FOR A LONG time been curious to meet Peter Dowdeswell but, although living just 15 miles away, I had not been to see him. It was probably fear. 'Ah,' said Doug Blake knowingly, 'the Muncher.' 'Animal,' said Tony Hackett down at the pub. 'The man's an animal.' Over the years an image had formed of a cave knee-deep in bones beyond which sat a hunched and terrible shape in the shadows.

'Excuse me,' I shouted brightly. It was a house on a council estate and beyond the privet hedge a snarling Alsation dog kept pace as I walked up and down the pavement. 'Hello, anybody home?' The front door opened. It was a cold, wet night but the man who stood there was naked to the waist, a huge man with more tattoos on him than a Pict. The Blue Man of Earls Barton. The Muncher.

He was not in a good mood. A national newspaper had taken his picture a week before, promising him £100 for his co-operation in eating eighteen fried eggs while sitting with live chickens on his lap. He had not received the £100. '*Wild chickens*,' he roared, waving his arms so that the eagles and the panthers writhed. 'They shat all over me suit.'

It was like one of those dreadful moments at school when you can feel the laughter boiling up in you until your eyes bulge, and dare not laugh. 'And the eggs already three hours fried. And them chickens pecking and shitting all over the place.' At that point I knew that I could not hold it any more, but then there was an explosion inside the room. Mrs Dowdeswell was laughing behind her paper.

'And they didn't even pay for the dry-cleaning.'

Peter Dowdeswell is a Londoner, born in Peckham, who moved to Northamptonshire 27 years ago. Formerly a bricklayer's labourer, he is 6 feet 1½ inches tall and weighs 16½ stone, not a fat man but with enough loose flesh on him to make the tattoos quiver when he is in a temper. What had he weighed as a young man?

'Sixteen-and-a-half stone.'

'Were you good at sport?'

'Nooo.'

They were wonderful noes; huge, arched and emphatic, each one a little longer than the one before. And with each his eyes got bigger.

'Do you drink much?'

'Nooooo. I'm teetotal.'

'Do you eat much?'

'Noooooo. I've just had me supper. Three sausages and chips. First meal I've had today.'

'Mr Dowdeswell, how do you spend your time?'

'Bingo.' But then a gap in his front teeth was there and he was grinning. 'I've never been anything in my life. I'm ordinary.'

But in 1974 there was a carnival in Earls Barton, and a contest for the fastest time in drinking a yard of ale, one of those long glass things with a bowl at one end which holds three pints of beer, and out of which, if you pause while drinking, the beer pours all over you. The record for this had been 1 minute 20 seconds. 'With spillage,' he said. Pressed into taking part, he drank it in 11 seconds. No spillage. As he was not a drinking man, he was unaware he had done anything out of the ordinary until he set the yard down and then there were all these faces staring at him in the square outside the church.

That night he was asked down to the working men's club and the barman put £10 on the counter and bet him to do it again. Ten seconds. No spillage? No spillage. The stress he puts on that is a reminder of what was to come, the stopwatches and the signed affidavits. Last year he drank a yard of ale in 4.9 seconds, in America.

He claims there is no knack, but he did grasp his gullet as though it were something quite independent of him, sinking his fingers into his throat the way a man might hold a snake, and brought it round to somewhere under his jaw muscles. The thing seemed to be flexible, and it was horrid to watch. 'It moves. Did you see that, all my system moving? The lot opens and I can tip it down. Didn't find that out until 1975, with the haggis.'

One curious feature has baffled doctors. He had seen his father drink 20 pints and at the end the old man was drunk. But after his yards of ale, Peter Dowdeswell was not drunk. He drank 25 pints of beer and a medical analysis showed that his blood reading recorded only one-and-a-half pints. In 1979, carefully monitored, he drank 76 pints of beer in sixteen hours, and again the blood alcohol level did not rise above a pint and a half.

'The Alcoholic Anonymous people, I think they were, they wanted me to go into hospital and split me open. But I drew the line at that.'

'So what happens then?'

'Dunno.'

Mrs Dowdeswell put down the paper and took off her spectacles to deliver judgement on her mate. 'He's just bloody abnormal,
that's all.'

One day a letter arrived telling him that he had been accepted
for the World Haggis Championship at Corby ('Lot of Scottish
in Corby'). Now he had not entered, but then neither had he ever
eaten a haggis. 'But the wife told me to give it a go, so we bought a
haggis and cooked it. I spewed it straight up, just like that. But
when it came to the night, with the papers and television there, a
man said "Ready, steady, go" and before I'd looked up I'd done it.'

One pound 10 ounces of haggis in 49 seconds. No spillage. But
then he said he had not tasted it. After that, he went on, people
were on at him to try other things like gherkins, grapes, pancakes.
There were contests in nightclubs. ('I've seen people choke, I've
seen them fall over') and invitations abroad (he took out a passport). The fat and boastful beat a path to his door to challenge
him and went away, chewing thoughtfully. He was hired by a
German lager firm as the world's first professional beer drinker,
but this did not work out. 'They wanted me to set records only
when and where they told me, but as I said to them, "If it goes
down, mate, it goes down, and that's all there is to it."'

In the front room he had begun playing his videos of American TV shows with frantic hosts who suddenly ran out of words
as a large, unsmiling man dropped boiled eggs into himself. He
began talking about the darker records, the glass. How could he
eat glass? Without a word he got to his feet and went out into the
kitchen. After a while there was the sound of breaking glass and
he came back with the remains of an electric light bulb in a bowl.

'Mr Dowdeswell, please... please don't.'

KER-AAK.

'I just bite 'em and chew 'em and swallow 'em. Like this. Yeah, I've cut myself. See this scar here, above the chin? Got a piece of a champagne glass through there, and a bloke had to get some pliers from his car to get it out. Lay on a bed of broken bottles once, face down, for 50 hours. People on me back. What do you think I ate? Soup.'

'What kind of soup?'

'The only sort I like, oxtail. I did 24 tins.'

He always eats a meal afterwards, and drinks water while attempting the record, but the water, he said, was only to slow him down if he thought he was going too fast. And the loose tooth? It had been a false tooth and he had lost it while attempting a record in America. He had eaten that and all. It had been an experience, he said. It had got him round the world, and his family with him. He had met a lot of people in his years as a public eating man.

'And they write it all down,' said Mrs Dowdeswell. 'I said to a chap once that there was no point throwing the frying pan at him, he'd only eat it. Saw that in the paper and all.'

But it was coming to an end, said Peter Dowdeswell, though it seemed the older he was getting, the faster he was getting. 'I go to a nightclub now and there are these youngsters with skirts up to their backsides, and there I am, sitting on my own, dressed in a suit. Sad really. I reckon I'll retire in six months.'

He claims never to have suffered ill-health, though there was a hernia once. No indigestion? 'Noooo.' And never any spillages, or dry-cleaning bills? 'Nooooooo. Apart from the wild chickens, the...'

And we were off again.

The Cricketer

I THINK I FOUND his grave last week. Everything added up, the date cut in the stone near the east gate, among the older graves, where I remembered seeing it, newly dug seven years ago, with the ink on the little wreath cards just beginning to smear. So this was his name. Mr Hands. Sydney Hands.

Napton Hill is an extraordinary geographical feature. Not part of a ridge, it rises so abruptly out of the Warwickshire plain it could have been designed as an exclusive viewing platform. The plain sweeps past it to the horizon, to Leamington and Rugby, and you have the feeling you could be on Mount Olympus here, with the gods. And you are.

It was March 1987, and I was walking through the churchyard, which is at the very top of the hill. I have loved this place ever since the time I was climbing it with my wife and daughter and came upon a two-ton Hereford bull ambling down the road towards us. A man likes to be reminded he can still do the hundred yards in 13 seconds and feel able to abandon his family at the drop of a hat. The bull's name was Ferdinand.

But on that wet March morning there was no sign of him, and I was walking among the graves looking at the inscriptions and coughing as dramatically as George Formby's father, for I was just getting over the 'flu. I had entered by the North Gate where the new graves are, and had been struck by the number of young people who had died in Napton. I walked round the church, noting the deep gouges in the porch pillars that some say were put there by our ancestors sharpening arrow heads, when I saw the wreaths in the rain. They were among graves where, as far as I could make out, there had been no other recent burials.

I don't know whether you read them, but there are few things in life more moving than the little hand-written messages. The balder the language, the more they tug at the emotions: 'Goodbye, Pop', 'Forever in our thoughts, John, Mary and the Kids'. You see those and you peer at another death, that of words. Only that morning in Napton there was an inscription of a different kind, a simple statement of fact I have not been able to forget; I don't think I ever will. 'The village team of 1926 is now complete.' Homer could have written that.

Who would they have been? Carpenters, labourers, farmers, perhaps the village schoolmaster. You will not find their names in *Wisden*, but that does not matter, as 60 years on one man remembered he had seen the gods saunter down that hill, before whom the teams of Warwickshire must have gone down like grass. I suppose I could have tried to find out about the cricketers, but I didn't.

It would have been too sad had I failed, as I probably would have done. How many now, in a village of a thousand people, have been born there? I doubt at the end of the 20th century there are more than a hundred; the houses become more and more immaculate, and the man who came yesterday shares in no folk-lore. You will not see anything like that inscription again.

I don't think a Christian wrote it; it had a quiet paganism as the writer implied that soon the wickets would be falling again. It made me think of those lines by Tennyson:

It may be we shall touch the Happy Isles
And see the great Achilles, whom we knew

The magic is in the casual pride of the last phrase, 'whom we knew' Sydney Hands. I should like to think he was a slip-fielder.

Relics of Wars Past

The Big Bang

MOST VILLAGES HAVE some private folklore: what the last squire did on Mafeking Night; how much so-and-so had to drink the night his car was found in the swimming pool; why the reading room was sold. So it is not surprising the inhabitants of Hanbury, Staffordshire, have something they, and it seems only they, remember. It is what they remember which is bewildering.

Men heard the bang in London; seismographic equipment recorded it in Casablanca, and in Geneva it was logged as an earthquake the morning the bombs went off 90 feet under the fields of Staffordshire. It was 11.10 a.m. on 27 November 1944, when 68 people died in and around Hanbury. Eighteen of them, together with the biggest farm in the area, 300 acres of it, were never seen in any form in this world again when between 3,500 and 4,000 tons of high-explosive bombs stored in a gypsum mine went off, the biggest explosion ever to take place in Britain. And be forgotten.

People assume a D-notice was slapped on, but when you go into the local pub, completely rebuilt after the explosion, the walls are lined with newspaper accounts and photographs of the debris. 'They stare at these and are completely baffled,' said the licensee.

Until Hiroshima, its blast equivalent to 20,000 tons of TNT, this was the biggest explosion in the world. Yet even though *The Guinness Book of Records* records the 4,061 tons of high explosive used to blow up the U-boat pens in Heligoland, it does not mention something that took place in England within living memory. And it was as though Hanbury wanted to keep its terrible hurt to itself. For years the only memorial was a framed list of names hanging in the church, and that included the seven villagers killed on active service in World War II. Then, four years ago, those who had died in the explosion were given their own memorial, a slab of marble provided by, of all people, *the Italian government* because seven Italians, all POWs, also died. But the real memorial lies a few feet beyond this: a crater so big you would be unable to recognise members of your own family standing on the other side. At 11.09 a.m. on 27 November 1944 that crater did not exist. A minute later it did.

'See that air shaft?' said John Hardwick, a retired civil servant. 'A chap called Bill Watson was last up that from the mine and when he got out, he looked around him and didn't know where he was. It wasn't shock, it was because the landscape he walked through every morning was so changed he no longer recognised anything.'

Hardwick, a farmer's son, was 21 when the blast happened. He was working in a field about half a mile away when he saw a 2½-acre wood go up, rising as steadily as a Saturn Five, until the trees were lost to sight. Farmers ploughing in subsequent years found some of the trees, only they found the roots first, then the trunks, as though these had been thrown like darts.

Roy Gregson, a retired farmer, was seventeen. 'Yes, I remember the sound. It was an enormous HOOOOOMP and up she went... and up... and up. The sky went black as the soil went up and I could see boulders rolling about up there, boulders in the sky.' A piece of alabaster weighing 20 tons came down three-quarters of a mile away.

Some died instantly, blown to bits, including an insurance salesman who had been on his rounds. Years later, Staffordshire County Council announced its intention of turning the crater into a tip, estimating, in its sensitive way, that 20 years of rubbish could go into that. But people objected on the grounds that the crater was a mass grave. Men, animals, machinery and buildings disappeared into its 150-foot depth, and all that was left when the sun came out again was a piece of mattress on the edge. They worked out who had gone only when these people did not reappear, and a local police sergeant walked in front of the earth-movers day after day.

Some died minutes later, when a reservoir holding 6 million gallons of water gave way. The mine was at the foot of the escarpment; reservoir, farm and Hanbury were at the top, so water, mud and stones rolled downhill, breaking into the surface buildings of the mine, killing 27 men there.

Chance played a part in some deaths. The farmer at Upper Castle Hayes was on his way to market, but had stayed on at the farm because a delivery of grain was late. He did not die in the explosion but in the wave of rubble that engulfed the car in which he and his wife were sitting.

'We didn't realise people had been killed,' said John Hardwick. 'They used to test the odd bomb, and we were used to explosions, so the first thing I did was to see whether the cattle were all right. I began to walk up to the village and met one lady leaning over her gate, and I could see from her face that she suspected the worst, for her husband was in the mine. He was dead, and they had seven children under twelve. She still lives in the village.'

He then began to see the scale of the damage: roofs had gone, all the chimneys, the pub was down, and the village hall, a wooden structure, had been blown into a field. And all the time news was coming in, that Upper Castle Hayes farm had gone, so it was becoming clear that what they had feared for some seven years had in fact happened; the entire bomb stock under the hill had gone up.

Hanbury is on an escarpment known as the Stonepit Hills, which have been quarried for alabaster or gypsum for as long as records exist. In the church lies a twelfth-century knight, Sir John de Hanbury, 'the oldest alabaster and cross-legged knight in chain armour in the county, possibly in the country'. Heated to remove water, this rock yields plaster of Paris, and in the late 1930s as many as 75 men were employed in the mines at the foot of the hill. But some workings were not used, so at this time the Air Ministry began moving bombs into the hill. After all, there was 90 feet of rock and earth above, to which was added a 2-foot 6-inch concrete lining. You would have thought such a store invulnerable, yet it had some odd features, to start with, the operational mine next door; but the planners thought the natural wall between them, varying from 15 feet to 30 feet in thickness, would absorb any blast.

Then again, it was not just a bomb dump. Bombs were not only stored here; they were also repaired whenever one was retrieved that had not gone off. And the repairs were carried out in the store itself, the equivalent of opening a welding shop in an oil refinery. A man who worked there remembered, 'It was like Aladdin's cave. You went from one cavern to another by passages ablaze with electric light. In the dark corners of the caverns you could see faintly the tiers of enormous HE bombs.' Some of these were 4,000-pound high-capacity bombs, the heaviest and most delicate in use, demand for which ran at 100 a day in late 1944.

For what nobody had anticipated was the strain an all-out European war would put on such a place. In the months around D-Day some 20,000 tons of bombs were being moved in and out each month, and John Hardwick remembers being told that this figure was its maximum capacity. Had that amount gone up, it really would have been Hiroshima in England.

And there is more. They were short of staff, the senior appointment at the dump having been vacant for two months. So, incredibly, 194 Italian POWs had been recruited, although, with Italy out of the war, they were known as 'co-operators'. None of these men had any experience of working with explosives, and afterwards were at first made the fall-guys. Then, as more information came out, it was revealed that the police made no checks on anyone entering the tunnels, except for smoking materials; this allowed people to talk of sabotage.

So what did happen? You will have gathered that anything could have happened at any time, and even now new theories are being floated. There was an article in the local paper which suggested that the dump had been bombed from above, which is absurd, considering the amount of earth and concrete that would have had to be penetrated.

What most people now believe is the statement made to a Services' inquiry by an armourer who was just leaving the caverns and so survived. He said he had heard a small explosion first, and only after that did the whole lot go up. But shortly before this, he had seen one of his colleagues using a brass chisel to remove a broken detonator from a bomb that had been returned. The use of such tools was expressly forbidden.

In the caverns, 26 men died instantly in the blast. In the farm above their heads, five farm workers and the farmer's sister-in-law were all killed. In the working mine next door, five men died from carbon monoxide poisoning; others made the long climb up the air-shaft to safety and a world in which the top-soil had gone from 1,000 acres of land, being scattered throughout the countryside. Some of it had gone up to 11 miles away, and what was left looked like the Western Front — only the Western Front became what it was after years of bombardment. This was instantaneous. There was so much mud and so many craters that they left the dead animals where they lay, and in the spring collected the skulls and ribcages left by the foxes. The stench was terrible.

Where the farm had been was a smoking crater half a mile long, 300 yards or more across, of brown glistening sub-soil. Fifty years on, fir-trees have managed to take root, and although for decades no birds sang there and there was a terrible quiet, now I heard the croak of a pheasant from somewhere in its depths.

I was walking towards the crater with John Hardwick and Roy Gregson. The county council, having given up trying to convert the crater into a rubbish tip, has suddenly become aware of its tourist potential and laid little paths for visitors. But mostly it is the villagers who walk them. As John Hardwick explained, while they would like people to know what happened here, they have no wish to see the busloads come to gawp. 'For years this was a moonscape,' he said. 'Because the top-soil had gone, there was no end of attempts to drain the fields, only nothing worked. They were trying to make land out of something which wasn't land any more.'

The Ministry of Defence is still around, its yellow warning

notices about unexploded bombs on the other side of the wire
beyond the new paths – although what bombs would be left unexploded when 4,000 tons of high explosive goes off is a mystery.
Now that the memorial is in place and paths laid, its civil servants
are planting trees along the lip of the crater.

We stared down into the crater, which covers an area of 12
acres. 'The more you look into it the bigger it becomes,' said Roy
Gregson. 'It's the extent of it.' Down below, someone had laid out
a long straggling cross in white alabaster stones, the grass around
it threadbare. 'You must remember it was war-time,' said John
Hardwick, 'it took three or four days for us to realise just how
many had gone. Overnight this was a place of widows and
orphans. And it was such a small village.'

One school (closed). Two pubs. A post-office. A church. And a
crater. That is all there is to Hanbury.

But there is no mystery as to why its tragedy was forgotten. 'It's
quite extraordinary what gets overlooked during a world war,' said
a spokesman for *The Guinness Book of Records*. The Allies were on the
Moselle and every day the bombs were falling ('Tremendous
Explosion at Nuremberg') when the war came to Hanbury. The
coroner recorded a verdict of 'accidental death caused by an
explosion on Government property', and the manager of the mine
kept a black suit in his car for two months as the corpses were
found. The school was a mortuary and one of the ladies washing
down the bodies found that the first of these was her husband.

As John Hardwick said, it was such a small village.

Bunker

I N   A   L E A F Y   B I R M I N G H A M   suburb, in the sort of road where no one walks and where learner drivers practise three-point turns, a house is up for sale. Not the freehold, just the thirteen years of a lease left to run on a house where nothing terrible ever took place and no famous man lived. Yet we were there the same afternoon as Sky Television, which is not in the business of ogling Edwardian brickwork. Or walnut panelling. Or even gardens. We were all there because of something which for the last 36 years has been under the garden.

Sandwell Metropolitan Council is selling Number 8 Meadow Road, Edgbaston, on behalf of the West Midlands Fire and Civil Defence Authority, and is inviting sealed bids in the region of £250,000. The council has provided a long prospectus, indexing in some detail the floor space and the bathrooms, but at the very end, after the garages and the stables, there is a hurried entry, where no square feet are given. 'Underground bunker. Comprising an extensive range of rooms suitable for a variety of uses, subject to planning permission.'

This, in the early days of the Cold War, would have been Birmingham's Führerbunker. From here the cinder which had been the city would have been administered. It is the first time a major nuclear shelter has been put up for sale.

'Actually we regard it as ancillary to the sale,' said a man from the Estates Department. 'So we haven't bothered to reference it in terms of square feet. How big is it? Oh, it's huge.'

The only clue to dimensions comes in the lettering on the prospectus map where, just as on mid-nineteenth century maps of the African interior, there are no boundaries, just large letters. 'We must be talking seriously big bunkers here,' said the photographer.

The cold air hits you first, and a mustiness. You go down the steps under the brambles (there are three entrances) and there is a long corridor leading to double doors, beyond which it continues. Near the double doors is a brass plaque dated September 20, 1954, which records that a long-dead Home Secretary cast a portion of the concrete in its construction.

And for a moment you feel like Caernarvon and Carter peering into Tutankhamun's tomb, for everything has been left as it was in readiness for the emergency which never came, ready for those 'specific persons' able to get here in those last five minutes. The store-rooms full of mattresses and camp-beds, the sacks of gas-masks, the projectors with the spools of film enticingly titled 'Radioactive Fallout'. The addressing machines. The addressing machines? Presumably the specific persons, unable to break with the habits of bureaucratic life, would have gone on writing letters down here, but to whom?

'This place has been used as a store-room for the last few years,' said John Edwards, chairman of the West Midlands Fire and Civil Defence Authority. Councillor Edwards, with his seven-year-old twins, was making his first visit. A Labour councillor, he walked through the rooms as sternly as a bishop in an abandoned knocking shop, and even more sternly resisted the blandishments of the photographer to pose in a gas mask. His little boys romped in this great wonderful burrow.

It would be possible to write a history of Civil Defence based on this place. There was the confidence at the outset in this gaily coloured poster: 'The occupants of this room have taken precautions against the three-fold menace of the Hydrogen Bomb. Heat. Blast. Radioactivity.' There were the detailed booklets with the sardonic tables ('Over 600 roentgen: almost immediate incapacitation; mortality in one week'). And then a remarkable invitation: 'Come for a relaxing weekend to the Welsh hills.' This went on; 'The exercise includes a major incident, involving search and rescue, first aid, communications, and ambulance recovery of casualties.' Bliss was it in that day to be alive. The leaflet concludes: 'Some time will be allowed for rest and relaxation if requested.' But as time passed, the tone of the leaflets changed, until finally there was this, after Civil Defence had been changed to Civil Protection (and what a world of difference is there), a leaflet entitled 'How to Improve Credibility and Regain Public Support'. On a blackboard in a lecture hall someone had written in large letters, 'Goodbye'.

There were many leaflets illustrating the tying of knots, so that after three weeks, the length of time they were expected to stay, those 'specific persons', as the Home Office called them, would have been able to hang themselves without much difficulty. There was also a very large teapot.

Inquiries so far have come from solicitors and accountants who see the house as so much office space; they have been vague as to what, if anything, they might do with the bunker. A perfect recording studio for a rock star, said the Sky soundman. Or acid house parties, sniffed Councillor Edwards. The caretaker Colin Billingham said only that he did not like to 'come down here' on his own. There was still the sense of what might have been, what might even be. I kept coming on heaps of flags which would have staked out a contaminated area and the holiday posters at which the specific persons would have stared, knowing these too had gone.

The bunker, said Councillor Edwards, was now surplus to their requirements. They had another one in Sutton Coldfield, an old Scout hut. An old Scout hut ? Well actually it was made of concrete, was above ground and had once belonged to some naval cadets. He had been assured that it met Government specifications but, speaking personally, he would rather be outside it than inside if anything did happen.

Built by Birmingham City Council, the bunker passed to the West Midlands County Council after the Heath—Walker local government carve-up. When that was wound up it passed to the West Midlands Fire and Civil Defence Authority, just like some vast Victorian sideboard passed down in the family which no one had the courage to throw away.

'We have this statutory obligation to plan for nuclear war,' said Councillor Edwards. 'The Government gives out £100,000,000 a year in grants for that. But we have no obligation at all to plan for peacetime disasters. Given that peace is breaking out all over Europe and jumbos are jumping out of the sky, I find that perverse.'

It was a cold April day, but the warmth hit us as we came out of the bunker. What a long shadow that sentence casts... we came out of the bunker. There were ghosts around us, the last of Hitler's court, but others as well, grey ghosts out of the future.

The Bomb Factory

THERE IS A MOVEMENT in the reeds, so slight it might have been the wind, then a head in water, a head as sleek and small as any which sat between the shoulders of a member of the Drones' Club. And so it is, that just before 3.00 on a November afternoon, I see my first otter in the wild in the British Isles. I think I must have said, 'Blimey!', for at such moments a man takes refuge in the expletives of childhood. Then suddenly something is creaking into the air, not 20 yards from me, something large and grey and unhurried. A heron is rising like an old turbo-prop airliner.

Fifteen minutes later, in woods now, a dead branch snaps underfoot, and there is a small shape dappled by the last sunlight. The fawn stares and in just three springs is gone. And I know exactly where I am. I am in the Garden of Eden.

I have signed the visitors' book at the security gate. I am wearing the hard hat with which I have been equipped, and I have read the 'Safety Instructions' leaflet over and over, lingering, like an examinee, on the rubric: 'Thoughtlessness may endanger your life, and the lives of others. Read and keep this document, it is issued to you for reasons of safety and security.' I am in the Garden of

Eden, where nitro-glycerine was made. I am in Britain's old Royal Gunpowder Mills.

In 1991, as part of its 'Options for Change' programme, the Ministry of Defence was preparing to sell off some of its many assorted properties. It was an extraordinary moment, for once the British military acquires anything, it very rarely lets it go, and change, as usual, had been forced upon it, in this case by Mikhail Gorbachev who had declared, 'I am going to do something terrible to you. I am taking away your enemy.' He was also, indirectly, taking away Waltham Abbey.

Some of the MOD's remoter sites would tax the efforts of the country's most imaginative estate agents to shift. But Waltham Abbey was the sort of property that developers conjure up on sleepless nights. Two hundred acres of it on the edge of London, within walking distance of the M25, within cycling distance of the M11. It breathed light industrial potential, houses as far as the eye could see, golf courses. The MOD called in the London develop-ment planners, CIVIX. On maps the site offered the even more heady prospect of a single development. Almost entirely sur-rounded by water, by the River Lea and by 4 miles of canals, it would be the perfect open prison, with middle-class conmen angling away the long summer afternoons. But there was also the greenery: why not a conference centre? All that was before the planners actually visited the site.

'I'd been in tropical jungles, it was just that I never expected to find myself in one in England,' said Dan Bone, a director of CIVIX. 'All it lacked was parakeets. We had to go away and buy machetes, just to hack our way in, for we couldn't see more than 20 feet in front of us. It was a year before I dared leave the tracks. *I was that frightened of getting lost in Waltham Abbey.'*

It wasn't just the undergrowth, it was what they kept finding in this place. 'I'm an architect by training, but I'd never seen buildings like these, all thrown about in what seemed to be gay abandon in the woods.' There were huge curving walls hung about with ivy, tunnels leading into darkness, and great fortifications, some of which were completely round in shape. Added to this was the crashing in the bushes which greeted their approach, the fluttering of large wings and weird cries. All that was needed was the odd arrow thwacking into a tree and some rhythmic subterranean chanting to have convinced them that they were in a lost world. Which in a sense they were.

It is not known for certain how long gunpowder was made in Waltham. The first recorded date is 1665, by which time a former fulling-mill had been converted for gunpowder production, but there is a tradition, perhaps fuelled by the irresistible combination of monks and gunpowder, that it goes back to Crecy in 1346, the first time gunpowder was used by an English army. Guy Fawkes is said to have got his supply there.

The site was ideal. There were the alder trees to provide the wood for charcoal, one of the ingredients of gunpowder. There was the water power from the River Lea to turn the mills and mix the ingredients, also the fact that from prehistoric times the river had been navigable (no one in his right mind would move gunpowder by road). The result was that this became the biggest gunpowder works in the country, so important that the government took it into public ownership on the eve of war with revolutionary France, some 200 years ago, and in public ownership it remained until 1991.

Canals were dug, but the barges floating in and out were like no other, being lined in leather and poled by men, for horses bolted and men did not. Steam power came and a narrow-gauge railway, the trains running on rails made of copper, and in places,

wood, to eliminate the possibility of sparks. By the late nineteenth century they were making nitro-glycerine there and gun
cotton for the new high-explosive shells. It was then that the
strange buildings went up, deep in woods already coppiced for
alder, the thickness of which acted as a blast shield. Each building, for obvious reasons, was as far as possible from the others,
which was why, when the first developers went in, they thought
there had been no plan.

But there was a plan, there always had been a plan. Huge
mounds were thrown up, the earth lined with brick, passageways
disappearing into the ground itself. The most spectacular of these
was the Grand Nitrator, 140 feet high, in the depths of which a
man sat on a one-legged stool, in case his attention wandered
for a second, overseeing the nitration process. Below him was
an oval pit of water, into which the nitro-glycerine could be
plunged if the Grand Nitrator threatened to overheat. Names
like this, and the goblin on the one-legged stool, are out of
fantasy, except all this was real and just half a mile from the town
centre.

It was another world in there, down in the woods. The workers
wore special uniforms made of calico, with no buttons or pockets,
the fastenings made of string. Every day a section of the safety
rules was read out to them, and once a month the complete set.
At the peak of the Great War, 5,000 people were employed there,
half of them women, and it is a remarkable comment on the
safety procedures that in all the 300 years of the mills only 200
deaths were recorded. With those there was very little left to bury.

By World War II, with Waltham Abbey in reach of enemy
bombers, its importance had declined, and in 1945 it closed as a
factory, only to open again the next day as a research establishment, specialising in every form of non-nuclear propellant. The

fuel for the Blue Streak rocket was developed here, the explosive bolts on jet-ejector seats, even Giant Viper, that enormous ribbon of explosives shot into minefields which was used in the Gulf War.

The last years were weird and wonderful, with many changes of name. ERDE – Explosive Research and Development Establishment. RARDE – Royal Armaments Research and Development Establishment. PERME – Propellant Experimental Rocket Motor Establishment. Most of these had no use for the bizarre buildings in the woods, so the green crept back. And not just the green.

Herons, attracted by the coppiced alder, flew over the wire and made their nests. Time passed and it became the biggest heronry in Essex, with the result that in the 1970s a secret government research establishment was, irony of ironies, classified as a Site of Special Scientific Interest, its explosions synchronised so as not to interfere with nesting habits. And somehow, under the wire, up the canals, came otter and deer and muntjak and rabbits, all of them safe within the security perimeter.

It was into this wonderland that the men with the machetes came, followed by men from English Heritage and the Royal Commission for Ancient Monuments. And then Whitehall's troubles *really* began. 'The men from English Heritage and the Royal Commission couldn't understand what they were seeing down in the woods. They'd never known anything like it,' said Steve Chaddock, later appointed the archaeologist-on-site. 'They said they needed to do an evaluation, but even before this, English Heritage decided to make it a Scheduled Ancient Monument, listing 21 buildings, one of them of Grade I, the same as Westminster Abbey.'

So it was goodbye the houses as far as the eye could see, goodbye the light industrial use and the golf courses. At the MOD, civil servants peered into the unknown, fearful of what might turn up next. There was the little matter of the waste from hundreds of years, all tipped into the canals, for you don't get the binmen calling when you run a nitro-glycerine factory. With English Nature, English Heritage and the Royal Commission peering over their shoulders, the MOD could not just send in the bulldozers, and the bill for decontamination alone came to £16 million in the end. All they got in return was £5 million for a tiny fringe of the site, some 10 per cent of it, where houses did get built. Powder Mill Lane, Powder Mill Mews.

But what were they going to do with the rest? The MOD turned *in extremis*, like most of the nation does, to the National Lottery, and this year the Heritage Lottery Fund announced that it was making a grant of £6.5 million towards the setting up of an Interpretative Site. For having finally worked out exactly what they did have in the woods, they thought they might let the public loose on the mystery. With a final grant of £5 million towards this, the MOD was shot of the whole thing. The Environmental Health people have given it the all-clear, and now only trifling little details need to be worked out, such as where the public will be allowed to go, or whether they will go alone or be guided, and where the entrance will be. Work has not yet started.

So you see it now as the archaeologists saw it, once the men with the machetes had been. The archaeologists made some strange discoveries, one of them, a man who had spent his life studying cast-iron aqueducts, of which just eleven survived in the whole country, finding another four within a few yards of each other in the woods. You come on huge rusted pieces of machinery in the most elegant of buildings (for when they built most of this place they would have found it impossible to build anything inelegant). You look down on the ghostly outline of a huge barge, just under the surface of the canal where it could be the boat which carried Arthur into Avalon. Some of it is on a huge scale, like the stone wheels 6 feet in diameter, each one weighing 3 tons, which were used to grind the sulphur, saltpetre and charcoal into gunpowder, and, their day done, were just left lying around as though some giant child had abandoned them. Nothing was ever thrown away.

You find old wharfs, towers, waterwheels, and then, as you penetrate deeper and deeper into the sort of jungle into which explorers disappeared, you find Aztec temples, the walls thicker than anything in a medieval castle. Then there are the dark places, the tunnels running into the earth. If you remember the comics you read in childhood, there is a remarkable familiarity about the whole place.

Only these were more terrible than Aztec temples. These were the Mills of Death. Some 95 per cent of the propellant for the shells on the Western Front was made here, the Dambuster bombs, and every other form of explosive and propellant before the atom bomb. What came out of this place killed millions, but all that was in another country. It is very weird that after all that, after these mills had stopped turning, that a man should think of this place as the Garden of Eden.

And so it is that just before 3.00 on a November afternoon, I see my first otter in the wild in the British Isles.

Airbase

I

THIS CONCERNS A MAN and an airfield. The airfield was his playground as a boy, and his enchanted place, for it had been so secret no one could ever tell him what happened there, until, 40 years on, the men came back. It is also the story of what follows if you see something in a landscape and, for once, stop.

North of Northampton, the B576 from Lamport to Rothwell rises to a plateau, a bleak place without hedges, its desolation made worse by signs that this was *somewhere* once: broken concrete, a few brick ruins. And the memorial. It is the newness of the marble which is startling, that and the fact there has been no landscaping around it. The memorial has just been plonked down beyond the fence around a lay-by. There are some fresh wreaths at its foot.

'We came here in 1954,' said John Hunt, of Dropshot Lodge, the farm you can see over the fields, 'and I was nine when I began exploring the old American airbase. It looked then as though whoever had been there had popped out for lunch. A few licks of paint, a few lights switched on and you felt the whole place would come to life again. It was eerie, I even came upon tyremarks in the ground where the planes had been slewed round.'

Six hundred acres of runways, hangars and towers over which a small boy exercised illimitable dominion, and once, clinging to the back of one of his father's labourers, was driven at 100 mph on a motorbike down the 6,000 feet of what had been one of Europe's longest runways.

But then in 1960 the lights came on again, so many of them that at night from the farm it looked like Las Vegas. The Americans were back, with three Thor missiles, and it was someone else's playground. John Hunt was fifteen and had bought a box Brownie camera from a boy at school. With this he took a photograph of the rockets, and suddenly there were military police all over Dropshot Lodge. And then it was 1962 and the Cuban missile crisis.

'All the rockets came up, and there were fumes coming from them. We hadn't seen that before. A man who had called to sell my father a tractor said, "Mr Hunt, the end of the world is at hand." My father said, "Shan't get much wear out of your tractor then."'

But he did, for by 1965 the rockets had gone and slowly the ground became farmland again. John Hunt married and succeeded his father in the farm. A huge man now, he remained as fascinated by the mystery as he had been as a boy, but all he knew for certain was that whatever had gone on there during the war, it had been, unlike other US bombing missions, always at night.

'This old chap was out ploughing at dawn when the planes returned. He stood up in his tractor and flapped his arms at them to show how cold it was, and one plane broke formation. As he looked up, a hand came out, and two beautiful gloves fell. Then another broke formation, and a third and a fourth, until the sky was raining gloves.'

John Hunt will not forget the day all his questions were answered. It was Sunday, 5 May 1985, the weather was terrible, and he was driving in the early evening to check on some cows when he heard a car revving in the lane. 'The last thing I wanted to do was stop, but I did, and I heard this American accent. "Excuse me, sir, I'm looking for an old airbase which was here," and this great wave of pleasure went through me.'

Since then, others have called, elderly now, returning, as John Hunt put it, like eels to the Sargasso Sea, as though they had to see just once again the place where they were first greeted by an officer, Tommy-gun in hand. 'You can get out now, but if you don't, and you once open your mouths . . .'. The man had patted his gun. 'All your folks will ever know is that you went missing in action.'

For this was the most secret American base in Britain, from which clandestine flights were made. They told him of people they had never seen before the briefing, and never saw again, a young blonde stepping out into the night over the Bavarian Alps, a French couple kissing on the tarmac who would be dead in six hours, the Germans having been tipped off.

And three years ago they stood by a Northampton lay-by, old men with their wives, some members of the French Resistance, for the dedication of the memorial to which they had all contributed. One thing you will find hard to get out of your mind is the scene chipped into its side, a black bomber and three cottages in moonlight, for when you look again the cottages are there, which were once someone's last glimpse of safety.

'I was ashamed of being an Englishman that day,' said John Hunt. 'There they were, the men I'd been waiting so long to meet. And it poured with rain.'

2

A badge, a thin enamelled thing, shows a white lion topped by a red star. It cost me 50p. I bought it from a chap with a suitcase full of the things and have put it in the wooden box my father made where I keep my treasures, not because of any value it may have, but because of what the hawker turned up in. He came in a MiG-29.

Such moments allow us to date our own lives. Someone comes back from a war, there is a murder in the next village; the post office burns down; and we remember where we were and what we were doing. But these are events. What is rare is when something allows us to identify a process already at work. This is why I bought the badge.

It was at the American airbase near here, the last air show that will be held, for the Americans are pulling out of Upper Heyford. The Dutch came, the French, there was the last operational Vulcan bomber, and then the Czechs arrived. They came in two MiG-29s. The US technical people swarmed all over them as soon as they were down, for this plane was the great threat of the Gulf War, and is the most manoeuvrable, the most advanced fighter-interceptor in the world. They marvelled at the roughness of the finish, the lack of electronic controls ('man, you really have to work in there') and the perfect aerodynamics. Each plane costs £10 million.

I was one of a crowd staring at the MiGs when two small men in light grey flying kit approached the barrier and grinned at us, showing rows of fillings. They put two boxes down, sat on some stools they were carrying and opened cheap suitcases, out of which they took some English phrase books and began selling not only cap badges but generals' stars.

I do not think that anything quite like this had ever happened before. It was as though Napoleon's Old Guard, still in being and undefeated, had pitched a booth and started selling off its Eagles. Or Hitler's SS had started flogging daggers and cap badges, not in defeat, but with the organisation intact but bankrupt.

The Czechs were such merry men. I pointed to the phrase book and the one with the amazing teeth laughed, 'Is good, is English book.' And all the time my eyes kept flitting to that terrible fighting machine behind him. Later, when they had stopped selling the trinkets that might allow them to stand a single round of drinks in the mess, one took off in the MiG and the thing punched a hole in the clouds. I watched this, playing uneasily with my new badge.

I told an American sergeant about the little stall and he said, 'Were they really? Whereabouts was this? I guess we should have a photograph for our records.' But they didn't, it was too sad for that. Only, of course, it wasn't sad at all. Good God, there we were, sunk in nostalgia for an Armageddon that hadn't happened. And it hadn't happened not because of military might or a sudden rush of morality, but because the books no longer added up. They have the bailiffs in; we just have them peering into the garage.

The last Vulcan, which unlike the MiG, really is a thing of beauty, took off. For a moment it was as decorous as a Victorian lady, with those long wings almost touching the tarmac – until the sound hit us. The American commentator could have been providing the sad-sweet soundtrack to a compendium of film comedy: 'And so Fatty Arbuckle fades into the sunset, loveable and innocent...'. Only he was talking about something that delivered H-bombs. 'And if no more funds are found, this could well be the last flight of this elegant old aircraft, once the pride of Britain's nuclear strike force...'.

The Vulcan came by at 300 feet, turned in salute and opened its bomb doors in a spectacle of quite staggering obscenity. It really did, and we all clapped, we really did, clapping what could have been the last thing in this world thousands of people saw.

3

About 10 miles to the north of this village, the A5, before that straight as an arrow, goes into a long bend for no apparent reason, except that in doing so it skirts a very large field. Twelve miles to the south-west there is a bustling town surrounded by wire. You might not think there was any connection but, as the old monumental masons used to cut, 'as the one is now, so shall the other be'. For the second time in British history the legions are pulling out.

That field was called Bannaventa when the A5 was Watling Street; a Roman town covering 30 acres. The town behind the wire is the American airbase at Upper Heyford, which some of you might live long enough to see also become 'old foundations, the stones of ruined walls and the like ploughed up'. It has just been announced that the bombers are going.

No one knows how a Roman town died, but there was nothing abrupt about it: fallen columns, public buildings used as a quarry, fires upon the mosaics and finally a place of ghosts to be avoided. But the end of Upper Heyford will be abrupt. A paragraph in the

national newspapers became headlines in the local weeklies...
'Massive Blow to Local Economy'. Over 5,000 servicemen and
women are going, with 7,000 dependants, possible as soon as
within two years. Add to this the thousand local people who work
there and the many more for the contractors employed by the
base, and you get the figure conjured up by someone of a £100
million a year loss to the area.

Nobody could have come up with anything as neat as that for
Bannaventa, for in its time the town *was* the area. It had been there
for over three centuries, the American airbase for only 40 years,
during which time it could for most purposes have been on the
moon. There is a frontier in Oxfordshire: cross that and you are
part of an alien economy. The slot machines take dimes; supermarket steaks are half the price they are beyond the wire, pork
spare-ribs twice as expensive. There is piped American television
and the flats have the verandas of small-town USA, homesickness
being held at arm's length here.

Yet rural Oxfordshire is all around (Flora Thompson's Juniper
Hill is just down the road); its roads go straight through the base,
so you can watch the baseball games on the lawns as you go by.
What makes it more extraordinary is the official fiction that this
is an RAF base. Road signs tell you this, and there is even an RAF
Commander, whose flag flies a few feet higher than that of the
USAF Commander, in spite of the fact that he has half a dozen
men under him, the other, 5,000. Thirty per cent of these live
behind the wire, the rest in rented village houses. It is the wives of
enlisted men who suffer most – out of the States for the first time
and able to afford houses only in remote villages. They keep their
curtains drawn day and night and their children we see as pale
faces in the backs of cars. They always look so sad, our guardians:
little families worriedly ordering in Indian restaurants, hesitating

about crossing roads, not understanding a word when you try to address them. 'Pardon me, sir?'

Of course, you get the odd top gun. 'Wadda we do? We drop bombs.' He informed me he had seen a lot of Britain. 'Only I get to see it *fast*, from 500 feet.' He was a funny man. He told me he flew all-weather planes, but when I asked what problems he encountered, he said, 'The weather.' Fresh from their desert training areas, some of them, he told me, had not even encountered clouds before. And I thought of Auden's Roman legionary on the Wall, with the rain falling and a cold in his nose.

I suppose she'll miss them, the solitary peace campaigner who lives in a caravan with a small daughter on the base perimeter, her cat a present from the military police. The Americans gave her lifts to the shops, and she sounds proprietorial when she talks about the rates of climb in an F-III. But not everyone will miss them. There is a village called Ardley, which has a Saxon church and was a quiet place until 1970, when the F-IIIs came. At take-off the F-III with its after-burners on makes as much noise as two jumbo jets, and some mornings there are two hours of continuous take-off. Ardley is just three fields away.

The MOD offered to buy some of the villagers' houses, but only on the basis of individual decibel readings, so one man might qualify while his next-door neighbour didn't. The latter appeared doomed to be as tethered to the landscape as a mediaeval serf, for who would buy a house in a dying village? But that threat is lifted, the silence is coming.

As it came to Bannaventa: so completely that for a thousand years men argued as to where this had been.

Fantasies

Up the Workers! (If We Can Find Any...)

NOT SO ORNATE as the *Book of Kells*, nor as old as the *Black Book of Carmarthen*, the *Book of Thame* is more mysterious than either. Its two volumes, each the size of a family Bible and fastened with pink ribbon, are kept in an Oxford library and are so fragile researchers are recommended to read them on microfilm. The Book is a report on the Oxfordshire market town compiled by its Communist Party in 1955.

That Thame ever had a Communist party is a great shock to its inhabitants. 'What?' said Mike Le Mesurier, the Mayor. But the fact that this party produced the most complete report ever compiled on a small town comes as even more of a shock to its members, of whom there were once eight. 'Never heard of it,' said Cecil Aldridge, chairman of a party formed in 1953 only to be dissolved a few years later. Mr Aldridge, a retired ambulance driver, alarmed at having his past leap from the phone, refused to be interviewed. 'I've gone off all that sort of thing.'

The mystery, though, is just beginning. Until six years ago, when it was transferred to Oxford for security reasons, the Book was at Thame library. But nobody at the library has any idea where it came from. 'I've been here ten years and it was always kept under the counter,' said the librarian. 'You must admit, the Communists did a wonderful job.'

Everything is listed: the local papers and their political leanings; 'quasi-military units' (these turned out to be the grammar school cadet force and the Observer Corps); chapels and churches (there is a detailed aerial view of the vicarage); with the names of every officer of every organisation in the town, including a Miss Lane, secretary of the Society for Promoting the Gospel among the Jews. The Communists even listed the Town Ghost, a priest said to do the washing-up at a sixteenth-century guesthouse.

Almost half a century on, the *Book of Thame* offers a unique insight into the pre-occupations of a Communist cell in the middle of England at the height of the Cold War. Had it come to Thame, the Red Army would have known exactly where to drink (every pub is photographed), where to shop (every shop is noted, including the one run by a man who kept bees and also managed to fit in being the town undertaker), and when to be on the alert ('When the Church clock and the Town Hall clock strike together, there'll be a death in the town'). Ignoring Stalin's question ('How many divisions has the Pope?'), the local party went into great detail on the town's religious organisations. The sermons of a former vicar were listed, including one at Lent on the theme 'Beguiled. Beset. Bewitched. Beloved. Betrayed.' The Methodists, the Party noted dryly, were a considerable force in Thame.

Even more care was lavished on the affiliations of local papers, especially the *Thame Gazette* ('Whereas formerly it devoted many columns to the Tory cause, and less to the Whig, and very little to the working class, it now keeps clear of all contentious news

reporting'). Political organisations were analysed, like the Conservative Working Men's Club ('Most of their activity seems to be
the holding of smoking concerts'). Of their *bête noire*, the Primrose
League, sinister and in the wings, they noted wistfully, 'It naturally
has many supporters in high places, and so can arrange annual
fetes in high places.'

   The Communists themselves had to be content with meeting
in a school, until the authorities banned the use of schools for
political purposes, at which point they hired the Town Hall –
before their funds ran out. After this, one of their number, a
market gardener, lent them a garden shed. 'We also met in each
other's houses,' recalls Celia Yeates, who, as the beautiful Celia
Prosser, then 23 and made to be photographed against the dawn
by Eisenstein, represented Thame, unknown to its inhabitants, at
the Fifth World Festival of Youth in Warsaw in 1955.

   'You weren't a Communist, were you?' asked her husband, looking up from his evening paper.

   'Of course, don't you remember?'

   'I played a lot of cricket in those days.'

   But his wife remembered her youth in a Communist cell. 'I can
recall my father Charlie Prosser and Will Warren, both members,
talking about spying. Will said he would pass on secrets if he
thought they would be of benefit to mankind. And my father said
he would, too. The only thing was, my father was a builder and
Will a printer. They didn't know any secrets.'

   Celia joined mainly to please her father, in whose office she
then worked. Not that it did her much good. Charlie Prosser
resigned in 1959 because the Communist Party wasn't Left enough.
He went on to become a county councillor, parish councillor and
a member of the rural district council, all at the same time. Later
he became a magistrate. Still, his daughter enjoyed her trip behind

the Iron Curtain, where she was unaware of any surveillance. In fact, she wished there had been, because she kept getting lost in Warsaw.

Mrs Yeates remembered old Comrades. There were Pat and Ken, whose surnames she had forgotten. Pat had been on the stage, Ken painted labels for some firm, and they once did a reading of a play the two had written. What was it about? 'Oh, Oliver Cromwell.' Then there were Will and Nellie Warren, who were vegetarians, which caused a major crisis in the cell when some well-wisher gave the Party a live hen for its sale of work (Will, after much debate, gave the hen back). Nellie used to weave, and had woven her own wedding dress. They also crystallised their own fruit. One of their two sons, Mrs Yeates recalled, ran away from home because there was too much politics in it. The other crisis, apart from the hen, was over the Red Army's invasion of Hungary.

When she married in 1958 and moved away, she lost touch to the point where, meeting Chairman Aldridge in the street, he affected not to recognise her and said he had no wish to be reminded of the old days. But in 1955, before the hen and Hungary cast their respective shadows, the future seemed assured. There were CND marches and there were discussions, at one of which Celia Yeates heard Will Warren say that, while Communism might not bring them immediate benefits, it would in time make their lives happier and more fulfilled. She recalls, 'He and my father were very humane men, more like Christians really. And Will knew so much about the town. I'm sure it was him, I'm sure Will Warren wrote the Book.'

It starts like a 1950s documentary film. 'Unsung, and unknown to most people, Thame is a market town on the boarders [sic] of

Oxfordshire...'. But despite the odd misspelling and crossings-out, its aims are epic. 'We have tried to depict the kind of person, influenced by Thame, who has made Thame what it is, and to indicate the people who are making Thame what it will be tomorrow...'.

And then the march past begins: Mrs Badger, secretary of the Folk Dance Club; Mr Tranter ('an optician of some renown'); a Mr Castle, who, at the unveiling of the memorial to Charles I's opponent, John Hampden, declared, 'We can regard him as a fore-runner of that great body known today as the British Legion'; also a remarkable, if unknown, bridegroom-to-be, who hearing his own banns being read out and being asked if anyone had any objections, stood up and objected himself ('Strange incident in church').

The town's secrets were explored, like the classified work which went on in a shed behind the Black Horse, where gliders with a 2-foot wing span were built. These were 'pilotless', reported the *Book of Thame*, not stopping to speculate on how a man might have fitted into such a small aircraft, 'and were towed by a Mr Eric Humphries at speeds of 120 mph in his Lagonda.' But Thame on the whole was a great disappointment to its Communist Party. 'It cannot be said that Thame is a hotbed of political controversy...' the Book noted.

Still, its compilers kept a beady eye on the Conservative Party ('It now controls the town as far as political parties are con-cerned'), an even beadier one on Labour ('at the moment they do not appear to be active at all, but will doubtless reappear at the next election'), and the beadiest of all on the Primrose League, 'that agency of darkness (Mrs F. Bowden, Dame President)'.

But history didn't call – in fact, it never really did in Thame. Even in 1929, when it was thought that some 200 hunger marchers from Lancashire were about to pass through the town, they never turned up. The man who owned the town cinema went on showing only those films he himself wanted to see (and not *The Battleship Potemkin*), there were meetings of the Motorcycle Club, ('almost all the members, whose average age is somewhere near 22, possess and ride motorcycles') and the Town Ghost went on doing the washing-up. The chroniclers of Thame were reduced to such bizarre news items as the car which ran over a chicken in the town and, in so doing, squeezed out an egg.

But at the end of the second volume there was a vision of the future when Chairman Aldridge decided to stand for the town council, and the *Book of Thame* has his manifesto. He called for more sports facilities in the town, also a maternity ward in the cottage hospital. Whether he got them, and was elected, is a mystery, as is the end of the Thame Communist Party.

All that is known is that when, in 1962, Dennis Manners, a would-be Communist, now a retired agricultural contractor, moved to Thame he found no trace of the Party. Like the Gladstone League and the United Nations Association, the passing of both of which they recorded, the Comrades had gone and their own book does not record their passing. The *Book of Thame* alone survives, like a ship's log found in the ice-cap of its dreams.

The Duchess

S HE HAD LIVED in a flat for a year. It was the first time she had done so, though not many members of the human race (or of its sub-species, estate agents) would call a Park Lane penthouse a flat. But to Margaret, Duchess of Argyll, anything with two bedrooms (a third has had to be set aside to accommodate shoes, clothes and press cuttings) represented the most abrupt change possible in lifestyle, short of jail or a tent. The human drama of it would not entirely overwhelm a hill farmer, watching the autumn rain close in, or a young couple trying for their first mortgage. No matter. It had not occurred to Her Grace that the world would be anything but fascinated by the fact that, after 30 years, she had found her Grosvenor Square house too large.

In the past the world always was. The young debutante Margaret Whigham in the 1930s announced her engagement to the Earl of Warwick, and it made headlines. The young bride Margaret Sweeny almost died in childbirth, and it was on the newspaper placards. Cole Porter's hit *You're The Tops* singled out human achievement, the Louvre, the sonnets of Shakespeare, the Mona Lisa, and

> You're the nimble tread of the feet of Fred Astaire,
> You're Mussolini,
> You're Mrs Sweeny,
> You're Camembert.

With her divorce from her second husband, the Duke of Argyll, the Duchess received the kind of press attention reserved for a war front. I was at University and we talked a lot about the Duchess of Argyll. She had entered folklore.

'I was known long before that,' said the Duchess coldly.

She had been married and divorced twice, given birth to two children (Brian and Frances, now Duchess of Rutland), travelled much and met many people. Apart from some months in the American Red Cross in London during the war, she had not worked. Yet her cuttings file in the library of the *Daily Telegraph* occupied three large folders. 'The *Express*, I am told, has five,' said the Duchess, and the commas clicked into place like rifle bolts. She had written an autobiography, *Forget Not*, and there were 400 names in its index, most of them people who were famous and/or very rich.

'Haven't you read it?'

I had to admit I had not, then; but that I had read the cuttings. The pale face seemed to close on itself, and it was like a submarine about to dive. 'My book is much *nicer*,' said the Duchess.

It is. *Forget Not* is an amazing, breathless book. Her Grace comes over as a little friend to all the world, much sinned against, but totally cast down by each new sinning. Her first husband, the golfer Sweeny, runs after other women. Her second, the late Duke, becomes addicted to purple heart pills and leaves her. But she endures among the liners and the great hotels, helped by millionaires and film stars. Her world is softly crammed into an address book and is a charming, predictable place full of hosts. To visit Ethiopia was to stay with the Imperial Family and be given an armed escort against brigands. To visit Argentina was to stay with the grandchildren of General Rojas, who, says Her Grace, 'liberated Patagonia from the Indians'. Had he still been around, one feels that Attila the Hun's grandson would have figured in the photograph albums of Belgravia. Only once does a cold wind from outside blow through these pages. At dinner one night Her Grace confesses to anxiety over the miners' strike, and for the first time you sense the Goths gathering in the long plains. But she is consoled by a fellow guest, an oil tycoon, who offers her the coal of America.

But not all is charm within her world. The divorce casts a long shadow, when the Duchess underwent a character assassination in public, unique in modern times. She quotes the description of her by the Duke's counsel, the dying octogenarian Gilbert Beyfus. He said that at her birth good fairies had brought every gift, looks, riches, but that a bad fairy had also come: 'I can't withdraw the gifts showered on you, but I will give you my own gift. You shall grow up to be a poisonous liar!'

She was sued for slander by her step-mother and by her social secretary; her predecessor as Duchess of Argyll tried to get her committed to jail, as that famous title which once would have had 4,000 clansmen springing from the heather had the lawyers wriggling out of the woodwork. Her Grace, during the four years of petition and counter petition, became a sort of one woman Arts Council to the Bar. The divorce was reputed to have cost her £200,000.

It had everything: sex, money, titles, New York private eyes. There was even a Cabinet Minister submitting himself to intimate medical inspection in order to prove he was not the naked headless man in the photograph. At the time a leader writer on the *Sunday Telegraph* said that the Duke and Duchess of Argyll had done more for the established order than anyone in this century. He quoted Disraeli, that the revolution would never come until the upper classes started enjoying themselves in private. The Duchess wrote her account for the *Sunday Mirror*, the Duke his for the Sunday *People*. She had kept everything: the news stories, the gossip columns, the cartoons. It had, she said, come in very handy for her memoirs.

Oddly enough she remained fascinated by the press, probably in something of the same way that military chiefs are fascinated by their hard-faced counterparts on the other side. She took the *Daily Telegraph* and the *Evening Standard* every day, 'and sometimes one of the other rags'. She read them in bed up until 3.00 a.m. The gossip columnists returned the compliment, but the beautiful deb their predecessors courted had become their prey. They recorded with glee her association with a charity ball to help the poor of Mayfair, and her attempts to open her house in Grosvenor Square to tourists (the lawyers were there again when her lessors objected): 'They are invited to view the giant bed in which Her Grace slept, with, amongst others, the 11th Duke of Argyll.'

Her portrait by James Gunn, at 10 feet too big for the penthouse, was to hang in an art gallery in Glasgow. 'Not many people get hung in their lifetime,' said the Duchess proudly. But one paper commented, 'It looks like a woman who has lost her memory and wandered out into the garden unsuitably dressed.' To some columnists it was always open season on Margaret, Duchess of Argyll, so it was clear that there was much more to Her Grace than charity balls and famous friends. A footnote to an *ancien régime* she might be, but you approached the Duchess across a minefield.

She rose to her feet, apologising for the deep black she was wearing. She had just been to the memorial service for Norman Hartnell, an old friend. Sure enough, in the papers next day there was a photograph of the Duchess with Barbara Cartland and the Bishop of Southwark. In dusty rooms in Fleet Street men cut out the photograph and added it to the folders.

The first impression was of physical frailty, as it apparently was in the thirties. She was small and pale, and very attractive, dark eyes glittering in an expressionless face. The elaborate black hair and the lipstick were both from three decades ago, but Her Grace, becalmed somewhere in her sixties, could have passed for a woman 20 years younger; the lawsuits and the gossip had not left a mark. But in the room behind her was a portrait bust, and you noticed at once the hard set of the jaw. The sculptor had seen Her Grace as a formidable woman.

The penthouse was on the top floor of the Grosvenor House Hotel, filmy curtains blowing out over the rooftops of Mayfair from a room full of Chinese antiques, a photograph of the Duchess in her Coronation robes, and one of Paul Getty. On the wall was a large oil painting of Arcady.

When I first arrived I had asked her brightly whether it had ever worried her, not having ever moved outside a certain circle. 'Oh dear,' said the Duchess. It was a tone headmasters used, and I remembered it. 'I am awfully frightened this is going to be one of those left-wing articles.' I had been in the room for three minutes. The same thought must have occurred to her, for she went on, 'I can imagine what their lives are like; I mean, my father had tenants and I went to see them. They weren't so very different. I am not interested in other people's lives.'

Her father made a fortune in industry, and she was a deb. She seemed to like talking about that. 'It was three years of absolute heaven. It was such a pretty era, the men in white ties. I know there was a Depression going on, but in a funny way we were helping to give employment. We didn't drink. We didn't smoke. And we were always chaperoned. There was no question of us living with anyone.' She looked up. 'These girls now, they lose everything and they gain nothing.'

She thought at the time it would last forever, the lunchtime dates, the afternoon naps and then the long dances of the night. 'There were three of us, Rose Bingham, Lady Bridget and me. We were pretty, we were quite sophisticated and we were everywhere. We were like the poor. The press were our friends: Lord Castlerosse, Lord Donegall. They wore two hats, one the hat of a journalist, one that of a friend. Nowadays they wear no hats at all. But there was Society then, and we were it.'

Her father, she said, had been very strict over pocket money. How much? The Duchess looked at me. 'I don't think it's a good idea to talk about money, do you?'

Then came the early marriage, and the war. She spent her war in the Dorchester Hotel. 'Everyone did. It was the only concrete building in London.' Yet she had little nostalgia. 'That doesn't do anyone any good. I think the only thing I really miss is the music. They don't have big bands any more. But you can do without so much. Before the war you wore a coat with a big silver fox collar and a hat made of feathers just to go out to lunch. I don't think they should have revived things after the war. They should never have held another Royal Ascot.'

Some of the dresses she wore as a Bright Young Thing were on exhibition at the Victoria & Albert Museum, but it did not bother her that in her lifetime she was history. Her ski suit was there, her wedding dress, her Coming Out dress and the dress she wore as a debutante at her Royal Presentation. They had all, she muttered, been far too big and far too grand. Anyway, they would never have fitted into the penthouse. 'I was always an awfully good thrower-away.' She did not know how many dresses she had kept. 'I can't possibly tell you. I mean, there are bathing dresses and summer dresses. You can't count them all.' But she had had to set a room aside for them. 'I suppose you'll want to see that.' Over her shoulder she said, 'You'll find it very neat. I am probably the neatest person you'll ever meet. I always used to tuck my teddy bears in at night.'

It was at the end of a corridor, past Her Grace's bedroom, past a cluster of Osbert Lancaster cartoons commemorating the divorce and her travels on Concorde (she is very much for Concorde). 'Isn't this a divine common thing to have?' She indicated the sealed Cellophane bags in which coats and dresses hung like cadavers.

There were drawers of silks and chiffons and furs, racks of shoes, long rows of dresses. The oldest pair of shoes was three years old. 'I have really learnt to compress,' said the Duchess, looking round her clothes room.

'I change once a day. Of course I know what to wear. If you're going out to the park with Alphonse you wear that. Or this.' Alphonse was her poodle. It was said in one paper that he went to the park, all of 300 yards away, in a chauffeured limousine, though Her Grace did not own a car. At another time it was said that he wore a jewelled collar, though it had been bought at Selfridges, said Her Grace scornfully. Poor Alphonse, to have ambled on to the firing range. The Duchess kept her press cuttings in a large cupboard in the clothes room; she did not unlock it.

She had one servant, a maid who lived in and a cook who came in every two days. The cook was there that day as Alphonse was being clipped. The Duchess did not cook. She had never cooked. 'I can't boil water, and I don't want to.' She laughed at this, which was unusual, for the Duchess seemed to be without humour. 'I loathe kitchens. I hate raw eggs. I hate butchers' shops. I'm not interested in gardening, either. What bores me is going to dinner with friends who cook. You never see them. What would happen if I lost everything? Oh, I'd manage.' Inspiration seized her. 'I'd buy take-away food.'

The Duchess was enthusiastic about Mrs Thatcher, even, oddly enough, about the way Mrs Thatcher spoke. 'Heath's voice I couldn't stand. But Mrs Thatcher's I like. She's so normal. She's got a husband. She's not kinky, let's be thankful for that.' Mrs Thatcher has been praised for many things, but surely not for that before. Her Grace also thought Mrs Thatcher would 'fix the unions'. She herself dreamt of becoming dictator, in which case her programme would include the execution of terrorists and people who were cruel to children. Her state would thus have something of an Islamic republic about it. 'It's such a free and easy age. I read about people who live together for two years and have a child without marrying. I'm shocked it should be so open.'

She was not, she said, a tough person. 'I can be quite sub-servient. If they like golf, I'll walk the golf course with them. I've done the lot, racecourses and all. I do have a quick temper, and I never retract. But you can touch me in two minutes and I'm an absolute sucker. I've been crying a lot about these wretched Viet-namese. I'm heartbroken about them. My worst thing is that I can become too argumentative. I have strong views about cruelty to animals, to children and about social climbing.'

She thought she had had a raw deal from the press over the

divorce, but did not care any more. Invited to sum up her life, she said, 'A woman who's had an interesting and varied life; and who has grabbed every opportunity to have a varied life.' Invited to sum it up in one word, she said, 'Adventuress.' She must have seen some surprise. 'No, no: adventurous. Adventurous.'

The house she lived in for almost 40 years was some 400 yards from her penthouse. The Dorchester, where she spent the war, was 100 yards away. She had to dine at the Dorchester when she gave dinner parties, for the penthouse had no dining room: she said this with the glee of a Girl Guide forced to camp out in Park Lane. Her London was as small as a mediaeval village, and so it must always have been for people of her background. I asked who had lived in the penthouse before her.

'Arabs,' said the Duchess.

The Butler of Britain

I T WAS AN EXTRAORDINARY news item. With even Chinese restaurants – a reliable guide to the late 20th-century British economy – beginning to close (two in one year in the town of Brackley), and with public pay rises pegged, there was still one area of uncontrollable growth. Last year the Government managed to increase its drinks bill by 35 per cent, spending £15.6 million on entertaining itself and others. And in a Northamptonshire village an elderly gentleman closed his newspaper and settled dreamily back in his chair.

The MP Tony ('it's a disgrace') Banks and the latter-day Anabaptists who write *Sun* editorials, were in complete agreement ('Eat, drink and be merry! That's the Government's new slogan'). But fourteen years into his retirement, home-made wines at 17 per cent alcohol steadily fermenting behind him, the man who for three decades was the Butler of Britain smiled in the knowledge that whatever else had changed, it was still party time in the Gardens of the West.

All my life I had dreamed of meeting such a man. You find

them in the footnotes of history, men who are at the centre of
things, yet whose perspective on events is so different from that of
the great, the latter might be just bit-players in their own history.
Fate ruled I was not to meet the Chief Black Eunuch of the Turkish Sultan's Harem, or the two Brandons, father and son, who
were the seventeenth-century headsmen of Old England. But fate
did allow me to meet Bernard Pettifer, now 78, and, in retirement,
my neighbour.

For almost 30 years he held the keys to the state wine cupboard.
Governments came and governments went; and to him, deep
underground beneath Lancaster House, they were all just so many
brandies drunk and clarets consumed. He entered these in his
ledgers, just as in the harem above the Bosphorus, the Chief Black
Eunuch recorded the copulation of the sultans, and the Brandons
inspected the vertebrae of the lately great. Men rose and fell, and
to him they were of interest only if they insisted on Malvern
water or decaffeinated coffee.

You may remember Walter Pater's lines on the Mona Lisa –
'She is older than the rocks among which she sits: like the vampire
she had been dead many times, and learned the secrets of the
grave; and has been a diver in deep seas, and keeps their fallen day
about her ... and all this has been to her but as the sound of lyres
and flutes...'. So it was with him.

It is the Banqueting Hall in London's Whitehall, that huge
room through which Charles I stepped to his rendezvous on the
scaffold with the younger Brandon, and where now the Government and its guests are awaiting the arrival of the Chairman of
the Chinese Communist Party. All are high on the self-satisfaction
of being present at such an occasion and do not notice that the
white wine they are drinking will do their teeth enamel no good at
all. The Butler and I, we are drinking champagne cocktails.

Everyone else who is there has been invited by the Government, but I am his guest. His authority appears to be older than that of democratic government, and the champagne cocktails have been materialising on the quarter hour. I have already had five and am philosophical, staring up at, and occasionally managing to focus on, the Rubens ceiling. The Butler, ram-rod straight like the sergeant-major he once was, is also philosophical.

'They come and they go,' says the Butler. 'You meet someone who seems to be in charge of the world almost, then he's gone. I remember the Turkish Prime Minister Menderes. Charming fellow. They hanged him.' He nods distantly to Edward Heath, who nods back. Assistant secretaries are making small-talk to other assistant secretaries whom they meet every day and do not like much. William Rees-Mogg floats by, impassive as a balloon. But then there is the plop of flash-bulbs, the Chinese have come. Hearing a rhythmic murmur by my side, I turn, and the Butler, his face its usual impassive mask, is quoting Omar Khayam, his favourite poem: 'Sultan after Sultan with his pomp/Abode his destin'd hour and went his way.'

Together we toast the Sultans. And then he says something I will find difficult to forget, for history of a sort is being made around us — years of diplomacy have led to these handshakes and these toasts (the Chairman is drinking orange juice) — as the Butler says, 'Of course, you get a much better party when it's non-political; things are much more relaxed when it's something like the Olympics.' He stops, rummaging among his memories for other landmarks in his long career. 'Or the International Congress of Dermatology.'

It all began in what seems now to have been another world. In 1929 in Northamptonshire a boy was leading a shire horse through the rows of a ploughed field; the boy was young and the horse was very big. It turned, the boy was slow to react, and it trod on his foot. 'I ran home to tell my mother. I was very tearful, for it had been a heavy horse, and I begged her, could I go into service like my brother?' Also his three sisters, for that was all there was, the Land and the Big House, and that was all everyone on those flat acres thought there ever would be. The Butler's tale would be a sombre fable of the old world, were it not for its last strange twist.

Sixty years on, I know that Big House; I know its owner, and might have seen something of life on the other side of the green baize door, except there is now no green baize door. There are no servants either. Yet when Bernard Pettifer started in service there were 20 of them, and it was his job as Hall Boy to serve their meals. In the pyramid of privilege he was at the very bottom.

'I can remember my master telling a guest at dinner that his father had had 200 servants, and had taken to his bed to sulk when they raised Income Tax by two pence in the pound. I wasn't sure what he meant by that, for to a pauper Income Tax means nothing.' There was no expression on his face as he told that story. There rarely is, except when he bursts into laughter and looks like a small boy: the years of service saw to that. As a young man he did not once see a soccer match or cricket game, except when teams visited the Big House. He worked seven days a week, from 6.00 a.m. to midnight each day, and was paid £18 a year.

'What do I think about it now? As with politics and religion, I rarely talk about my old life, but at least I knew where I stood. When you go into the Civil Service, as I eventually was to do, everyone thinks he is in charge of you. In service you have no doubts as to who is. And there was one thing about the men in the Big Houses: they preserved old England – they preserved it as it was. You could say my feelings are complicated.'

It was only when someone left service and returned with tales of a world outside ('of men's work') that he began to question his lot. In 1935 he entered the remote and formal world of the Biggest House of all: he became sixteenth Footman at Buckingham Palace, where there were seventeen footmen. From here, when George V died, he made his first attempt to break away and join the police. He was turned down on the grounds that he had too many false teeth. So his life in service continued. He moved to Marlborough House with the widowed Queen Mary: by now he was married and his wife was a cook there. Then suddenly out of the East came a great wind which blew open the green-baize doors.

He went to war, and at Monte Cassino was promoted to sergeant-major, and was later offered a commission he did not take; he could not have coped with that. At no time during the war did he tell any of his fellow soldiers what he did in civilian life; he was too embarrassed.

The end of the war was the blackest time of his life. His wife and son had been evacuated to Rutland, and on the second day he was home the farmer turned up to say he needed the cottage they were living in for a farm labourer. So Bernard Pettifer turned farm labourer. Not being mechanical, he was given the roughest jobs, and his hands swelled until they were so bad his wife had to tie his boots for him each morning. In despair he went back to service in Marlborough House, and was there when the old Queen died, when he was pensioned off.

And it was then that the extraordinary twist occurred. He saw the job advertised of Catering Manager (One) in the Government's Hospitality Fund, and applied. To his considerable surprise, he found himself appointed the Government Butler, a job he did not even know existed.

His office was an ante-chamber to the State wine-cellar under Lancaster House, the best wine-cellar in the country, he says — and he should know. That in Buckingham Palace was bigger, but there was nothing of interest there. When we met he showed me round the state cellar, pausing at the two bottles of Mouton Rothschild 1953, all that was left, for no one has come up with an excuse for an event which would require such legendary claret. His duties were roughly those of his surviving counterparts in the big houses, except he was in the strange position of being in service without a master. 'With a master he knew how far he could go with you before you'd sulk or leave. Here you came up against so many personalities, some stuffy civil servant or a PPS who was a pig, a proper snob. You had to use diplomacy.'

But he had the wiles of the servants' hall on his side. A single sherry in his office, he said, did more to cut red tape than 500 letters. They were heady days, for in addition to the booze he was in charge of the government silver, and one day he reported to his superior in the Hospitality Fund that there were no proper table decorations for banquets. That afternoon the two of them spent £10,000 of your money, and mine, in the jewellers.

His world was Lancaster House, Hampton Court, the Banqueting Hall, Henry VIII's wine cellar in Whitehall, and the two Downing Street houses, numbers 10 and 11. The biggest change in his duties was when Harold Wilson came to power — a man he always liked ('He never called me anything but Mr Pettifer') but who would insist on strange parties with show business guests. 'I remember one of these. Everyone had gone except this actor, who was very drunk and kept telling the Prime Minister, 'Yer no bloody good, d'you know that?' Nobody knew what to do with him, so I went up and said, 'Excuse me sir, your car's at the door.' He was so surprised, for he didn't have a car, that he got up, and when I got him to the front door I kicked him out. He came from Liverpool.'

George Brown he disliked intensely. 'He never knew what to call you. "Leave that, steward," he'd say of an unopened bottle, but I didn't. I had to do my returns and make sure they added up.' He liked the old-style Tories best, he said, for he knew where he was with them, and they knew where they were with butlers. Some of the Labour people tried it on with him. '"Pettifer," this man said, "Try this wine, will you?" "A perfectly good Burgundy, sir." "Well my friends here say it's off." "That's probably because they think it's claret, sir."'

I met him when he was one year away from his retirement. This had been planned with the care with which he approaches everything, and the bungalow had been bought in the Northamptonshire village where he was born, but, after all they had been through together, his wife died suddenly before they could move in. That was the year before we met.

The interview had been set up by a magazine I then worked for, and as I pedalled my bicycle towards Lancaster House, I kept thinking there had to have been a mistake, for the idea of a government butler was pure Gilbert and Sullivan. 'Where d'you reckon on putting that bicycle, sir?' asked a policeman suddenly stepping into my path. Startled, I said I had thought of chaining it to the railings, but he shook his head and looked very tired. 'You put that within a hundred yards of this place and there'll be blokes inside having heart attacks.'

It was then I realised that everywhere I looked there were policemen accompanied by armed soldiers, and when I eventually got inside Lancaster House there were others staring into closed-circuit screens. I had forgotten that upstairs Rhodesia was being negotiated away. But then I was through the cordons and, in a lift, sinking through concrete like a bathysphere in the sea, at a certain depth of which there is always peace.

That was eighteen years ago and Bernard Pettifer's odyssey is complete. The bungalow he bought is in the village where the bell calling children to his old school is the only one he hears – he whose life was once full of bells. It is all behind him now, that little white cave where he agonised over the drinks trays of foreign potentates; and over Mr Wilson, who was polite; and Mr Brown, who was not; and Mr Heath, for whom once, at Trooping the Colour, he substituted champagne for the usual Pimms No. 1, knowing he loved champagne. 'What, no Pimms?' asked Mr Heath grumpily.

The 27 Troopings of the Colour are also behind him. And Buckingham Palace, where he was given six weeks just to find his way round its subterranean passages.

Yet none of his neighbours have been told any of this.

Ghost Train to Stalybridge

She is not any common earth
Water or wood or air,
But Merlin's Isle of Gramarye
Where you and I will fare.

I WAS EARLY. I SAT alone on Platform 3a at Stockport Station, a sort of half forgotten annexe to the main-line platforms, gloomily remembering what the lady in the ticket office had said in answer to my question when I bought my £1.75 single to Stalybridge. 'How long does this train take?'

'Let me see.' The service did not appear to be listed in the usual timetables, and the queue behind me was getting more and more restless so that when she finally said, 'Ah, here we are.' I would not have been that surprised had she announced she had found it in the *Book of Kells*. 'Twenty minutes.'

'Can I have a return?'

'Well you can, but that'll mean you catch a train into Manchester, then another back. *This train does not return.*'

A light rain was becoming mist as, on other, through, platforms,

some admirer of Lord Haw-haw called people with somewhere to go to, and places to see, to exotic Stoke and legendary
Cardiff. But on 3a, where the line ends, I stared at the weeds and
the rusting rails beneath me, and was a man at the edge of the
world.

Ten years ago there was an hourly service through the outer
suburbs of Manchester from Stockport to Stalybridge. Now there
is just one train *a week*. This leaves Stockport every Friday afternoon at 3.00, and does not come back, or rather, it does, but then
no passengers are allowed on it. Every week they disappear into
Stalybridge and what becomes of them is of no interest to the
railway company. You will not need reminding that there were
trains like this in Hitler's Germany and in Stalin's Russia, and it
does not help that the Stockport to Stalybridge is known in the
railway press as the 'Ghost Train'. But to Northwest Trains, the
company responsible for it, this is known as a 'Parliamentary Service'. By running it once a week the company is able to avoid the
lengthy, and costly, bureaucratic procedures which attend the closing of a line, even one that has outlived its commercial use.

There were, indeed still are, two stations in Manchester, the
one on the main line South, the other on the main line to the
North East, and until the late 1980s anyone needing to cross the
Pennines, from London to York say, had to change trains and
cross the city in the process. The Stockport to Stalybridge was
thus a link service between the two, enabling travellers to avoid
Manchester altogether, but for ten years now there have been
through trains from the South of England to the North East. So
a busy suburban link became a parliamentary service.

When this happens you enter a world meaningless to anyone
who is not a lawyer or an accountant, for there is no obligation on
a railway company to make a profit on such a line, a profit might

even be an embarrassment. All it has to do is provide a service which passengers could use if they chose, and the company has no interest in attracting them to something which long ago disappeared into the small print of railway timetable footnotes. Even finding it in these is something akin to the three-card trick... *Now you see it, now you don't...*

Thus North London Railways have taken up the rails between Watford Junction and Croxley Heath, so their Ghost Train is not a train at all but a bus which runs once a week *at twenty past six in the morning.* And there is one beyond this again. The 06.48 a.m. Derby to Sinfin Central train service, which once carried factory workers, is not even a bus, *it is a TAXI.* These moments of lunacy at dawn should long ago have been immortalised in film comedy, for you can imagine what the late great Will Hay, playing a taxi-driver, would have made of the farce enacted once a week at dawn in the forecourt of Derby Station.

'Sorry sir, you may not hire this taxi. Yes, I know the law too, and of course it is your privilege to report taxi drivers for refusing a fare. But this is not a taxi. It was a taxi five minutes ago, and it will be a taxi again in half an hour, but at the moment it is a train. It became a train at eighteen minutes to seven, and no, my name's not Cinderella, sir. I know it may not look like a train to you. I know it doesn't run on rails. But that's what it is, a T-R-A-I-N. And puff puff to you too, sir, if you don't mind me saying so.'

Apart from some local people and rail enthusiasts crazy enough to get up at these ungodly hours, nobody knows about the Ghost Trains of old England, even when, as in the case of the Stockport to Stalybridge, this is a ghost at tea-time.

'It's worth going on, if only for the station buffet at Stalybridge,' said Pip Dunn of *Rail Magazine.*

'Fair enough, but can you imagine anyone writing 2,000 words on a 20 minute train service?'

'We do that all the time here,' said Mr Dunn.

You will gather from this that the idea to ride the Ghost Train did not originate with me. It was something I agreed to do, then put off until finally it became an embarrassment. And so it was that having driven 250 miles, I sat gloomily on Platform 3a, watching as the rain thickened and the tower blocks of Manchester went out one by one.

'Afternoon.'

He was in his late thirties, a thick set man in a leather jacket and jeans, a haversack over one shoulder. I had company on 3a.

'Excuse me asking, but you wouldn't be taking the 3 o'clock to Stalybridge?'

'I certainly am,' said the man, sounding like Oliver Hardy.

'What for?'

This is the Policeman's story. He was travelling through Manchester, he said, he had time to kill, and, for old time's sake, wanted to see what had become of a train he had last taken 20 years before. No, he hadn't told anyone of his plan. People would think him mad, said the policeman. One odd thing though, there were just two stations on the route, and even when he had used the service regularly, he had never seen anyone alight, or waiting, at Reddish South or Denton.

'Just one question, do you love railways?'

'Oh yes,' said the Policeman.

It was five minutes to three now, and an elderly lady and what looked like her son had turned up. A guard came, his two flags protruding from a satchel. 'No sign of the train is there?' he asked. 'I don't know where it's got to.' Three o'clock came and went. At four minutes past, there was an announcement. 'For all those

awaiting the 3 o'clock to Stalybridge, we are sorry for the delay.'
Nothing unusual about that, it was what came next which was so
strange. 'The full extent of the delay will be given as soon as possible.' All other announcements about delays had given reasons
and times. 'Due to signalling problems the So and So is running
ten minutes late. We apologise.' But the station authorities themselves did not know what had happened to the Ghost Train.

'Is it usually late?' I asked the old lady.

'Yes,' she said.

And this is her story. It was all her fault, she said. Her grandfather had had a model railway in his garden, with trains big
enough to sit on, so, when she had a family of her own, her idea
of a day out was to take her two boys on a train. It did not matter
much where the train went, nor did it now when she was old and
they took her. Her bearded son listened impassively. She had
passed her enthusiasm on to them, she went on, and his brother
was even keener than he was. Most summers they went on the
Stockport to Stalybridge at least three times, in winters less. Why,
they had even met a lady on it once, who had actually wanted to
go to Stalybridge, someone with a suitcase.

'You haven't been before?' she asked me.

'No.'

'So you haven't been to Stalybridge Buffet?'

'No.'

She and her son exchanged glances, and the two smiled.
Stalybridge Buffet, I gathered, seemed to be some rite of passage
awaiting me at the end of the line.

'Here she comes,' shouted someone, and out of the mist came a
fussy little diesel, not only 20 minutes late but a train out of time
altogether, the line having never been electrified. I had not seen
one of these in 20 years. It stopped and some twelve people, most

of whom I had not noticed on the platform but who seemed to have been beamed down like the crew of the Starship Enterprise, got on. Only they did not get on the way people normally do, they piled on board, the old lady amongst them, like children on a school trip or soldiers going on leave, as though terrified they might be left behind.

I found myself in one of the two elderly carriages with three men who, to my amazement, told me they worked for the railways. One was a signalman, another an engine driver, and the third a younger man just about to join. All had come a long way for these 20 minutes to nowhere, one from Accrington, another from Reading, the third from Swindon.

'Why?' echoed the Engine Driver. 'For this. Listen.' He lifted his hand. The little diesel was shifting from side to side like a sprinter in the blocks, every bolt vibrating. 'Oh, you old mechanical thing,' he said fondly. 'That's why I come. This is *real*. It is one of the last Class 101 DMU's in service.'

'So you've been before?'

All three grinned. 'We come as often as we can,' said the signalman, a sharp man, his hair in a pony-tail, not at all the sort of chap you would expect to spend his day off crossing England to travel 12 miles on an old train. It was then I realised I was in the company of a species I had thought extinct, railway men who loved railways. I had met one or two in the old days, rural stationmasters who spent their lives growing roses on their platforms, ticket collectors more immaculate than Guardsmen, but had assumed their pride had been destroyed by privatisation and by its bleak new ruling class of accountants and PR men. So it had survived, not at the top, but as Rome in its decline had survived, in centurions still at their post peering across some frontier. As the poet Robert Graves wrote, 'A rotten tree lives only in its rind.' And I started to suspect I might enjoy my afternoon.

The brakes were released and with a lurch we were off. Peering into the murk, I felt a hand on my shoulder. 'You do realise you are on one of the highest viaducts in Britain,' said the old lady. 'In a moment you will see the Pennines.' The two of us stared out together. 'Ah,' she said, like Tommy Cooper when one of his tricks had gone wrong. 'No you won't.'

We came to a station and one of the railway men opened the window, something you can still do on this train. 'Anyone getting on?' asked his friends. He shook his head, 'No,' he said, as happy as any man confirming an article of faith. 'Hang on though, the guard has just got out.' They watched him standing in weeds waist high, an explorer in some lost city of the Incas. In all the years they had travelled the line, they said, no one had ever seen a living soul on Denton Station. But then people can grow up in Denton and not even know they have a station. My own cousin has. 'Are you sure you didn't dream this journey?' he said.

The green was all round us now, and deepening over hanging trees, neat suburban hedges, overgrown verges, a world of willows and elder. I did not have not a clue as to where I was, or later, where I had been, when I retrieved my car from Stockport and drove between factories to Stalybridge, a journey which, curiously, took me over an hour.

'See that?' the Signalman was pointing to a signal-box. 'That's Denton Junction, that is, until eighteen months ago the last signal-box in Britain with gas lighting.'

'Have you ever tried to explain to anyone your fascination with railways?'

'No,' said the Signalman. 'That would be pointless.'

'Put it this way,' said the Engine Driver. 'The train might be noisy and rattly to you, but that's why we've come. We work in an industry that's done away with smoke and which is now trying to do away with sound. Everything has to be silent and brilliantly white. We are here because modern life is wrong.'

The train pulled into Stalybridge, but when I looked back through the rain I saw that the destination indicator on the front cab said Ormskirk. By that stage I was prepared to believe anything, for by the time I turned round again most of the passengers had vanished, apart from the old lady, her son and the Signalman who were hurrying towards the station buildings.

The Buffet at Stalybridge is one of the few free houses in the rail network. A narrow little room, it has not changed much since it was opened in the 1880s, and still has an open fire. But that was not the first thing I noticed. On the bar was a barrel of home-made perry. Perry is my favourite drink, but in 40 years of peram-bulation through licensed premises I had not seen it for sale anywhere outside the pear orchards of Herefordshire, even there never in a pub.

'Oh, we always have a barrel of perry,' said the Licensee.

I had a pint, and it smelled of elderflower. The next time I went to the bar I saw they also did wheat beer. Wheat beer is that lovely white beer brewed in Belgium and Germany, but which in this country is difficult to get outside London. Wheat beer, my second most favourite drink, is something for which I have often driven 20 miles.

'Wheat beer, please.'

'What kind would you like?'

'Which kind would I like? How many have you got?'

'Eight.'

Men have always fantasised about Journey's End, the great good place where wishes are met. At different times, and in different cultures, this has been the Happy Isles, the Land of Cockayne, in Welsh, Afallon, the Isle of Apples, Brigadoon, the Blue Rock Candy Mountains: it is just that no traveller who looks for it can find his way there. But say there was a train out of place and time, a train that went nowhere and never came back.

'Usually we have 20 guest beers a week,' said the Licensee.

'I knew you'd like it here,' said the old lady. Here at the quiet limit of the world's end.

Dead Writers Society

OT EVERYONE CAME to lunch. The Thomas Lovell
Beddoes Society, having found the nearest pub, disap-
peared into it. They felt they owed this to Thomas
Lovell Beddoes, explained their chairman, a kinsman. 'He was a
drunk who was thrown out of five European countries.' The
Dylan Thomas lot, as might be expected, had not turned up, and
John Clare had wandered off somewhere. But the Brontës came,
from moors where the footpath signs are now in Japanese, also
Fanny Burney and Jane Austen from the rectories, sitting together
straight-backed and demure at the tables reserved in a café in
Tesco for lunch. In Tesco... you might like to think about that for
the moment. Book a table at Le Gavroche and nobody would
think you in the least odd. It is when you encounter people who
have booked tables in Tesco that the suspicion comes you are
among no ordinary humankind.

A rosy-cheeked countryman from the Richard Jefferies Society.
Ageing lads in tweeds sporting the Housman Society tie of a

team ploughing, and a lady from the Mary Webb Society, small, sharp-featured, unsmiling, looking as though she could spot doom at a hundred yards. It was a march past of the enthusiasts, only one man's enthusiasm is not another's. In Tesco, Sherlock Holmes confessed that he had never heard of John Clare, William Barnes, Beddoes or Ronald Firbank ('Isn't he an actor?'). Douglas Warren, representing the Sherlock Holmes Fellowship of London, looked up from his shepherd's pie. 'I'm not a literary man, I'm a civil engineer.'

The Alliance of Literary Societies, representing a collective membership of some 20,000, meets just once a year, but for that day, that one remarkable day in a Unitarian chapel in Birmingham, English literature is laid out in front of you like a stock market index. Who's in, who's out, whose reputation is enjoying a tidal wave of popularity (prompted by such events as Colin Firth emerging from a lake in a diaphanous shirt in the BBC's *Pride and Prejudice*), it is all there in the number of books on the little stalls, the opulence of the journals published by the various societies, even in the alacrity, or the lack of it, with which members have paid their annual subscriptions. 'Not heard from the Edward Thomas Society this year,' said Bill Adams, the Alliance secretary. 'He can't be doing too well.'

The Eng. Lit. industry, however its academic practitioners present it, is basically an exercise in share pushing. You find your writer, preferably dead, even more preferably forgotten, then you promote him through little essays bristling with footnotes; 'The effect of Welsh metrical form on Dylan Thomas'; 'Arthur Machen, a late Gothic phenomenon'. And it doesn't matter that Dylan Thomas never read a line of Welsh poetry or that Machen once calculated that 40 years of writing had brought him £635: sleek careers can be founded on them. It matters even less that your writer may be just as forgotten afterwards, for who can measure popularity?

During last month's meeting the Alliance held a raffle and the prizes were books contributed by the different societies; a Virago paperback of Mary Webb, a critical analysis of Rider Haggard. Both were new. But among them on the table was *Portrait of a Village* by Francis Brett Young. I picked this up and turned to the publication date, 1957. Not new. One society had not provided a book at all but a bottle of wine, probably the Thomas Lovell Beddoes lot, the chairman of which had told me it had been a toss-up between forming a fine wines society and one to honour the poet. His being in print is the least of their worries.

'I know it sounds terrible but I haven't heard of some of these chaps, let alone read them,' said Mr Adams. 'Who was David Jones?'

'He was a poet who went to bed for the war,' I said. 'He'd been on the Western Front, and when the Second World War broke out felt he had had enough.'

The Alliance was founded in 1973 when Bill Adams' wife, Kathleen, incensed to hear that one of Charles Dickens's houses was about to be demolished, wrote a letter to *The Times* suggesting literary societies join together to provide a corporate voice. A dozen societies wrote in and for fifteen years, with Mrs Adams as secretary, this was the Alliance. They had no money, no committee, but they had an effect. 'A petrol station was going to be built in Nuneaton in Warwickshire next to George Eliot's childhood home, and they all wrote to the borough council. Now a council doesn't mind in the least if local people call them philistines, but they mind very much when people from all over the country do. We heard no more about the petrol station.'

At that stage it was a self-help society. Things changed dramatically in 1989 when the Birmingham and Midland Institute offered the Alliance a home, at which point Mrs Adams bowed out and her husband, a retired civil servant, took over. Bill, a cheerful red-faced gentleman, had a list. Every literary society he had ever heard of or read about was on his list, and Bill wrote to them all.

Some writers attract followers as jam attracts flies. There will always be a Byron Society for there will always be wistful upper-middle class ladies with time on their hands. There will always be large men with moustaches to form the Kipling Society, and passionate ladies trying to contact Emily Brontë by setting their palms on her grave. Most may no longer be young but their enthusiasm is far beyond that of the teenagers who follow pop stars. These are the ultimate fans.

A curator of Hardy's cottage once told me that a few months after he and his wife moved in, a letter came from three men asking if they might stay the night. They were planning to re-enact Hardy's visit to Cornwall and his meeting with his first wife, which became the poem 'As I Set Out for Lyonesse'. He and his wife were so startled by the request they agreed, and watched incredulously as three men stumbled out into a winter dawn, lurching through muddy fields, for they avoided 20th-century roads, to catch whatever westward train at Dorchester that the President of the Immortals, and British Rail, still provided.

Enthusiasm for the Alliance was never in doubt. It was just that the societies were fragmented until Bill Adams wrote. And wrote. And wrote again. Eighteen months ago there were just 37 societies in the Alliance. Now there are 73. Members of one join another or go on to form a new one of their very own. Their constitution was drafted by Mrs Adams who, after 25 years as chairman of the

George Eliot Fellowship, knows more about such things than anyone living. The result is that literary societies are rising out of the earth as soon as a writer is in it, and this summer the Philip Larkin Society holds a conference at the University of Hull which it has called 'New Larkins for Old'.

Not everyone replied to Mr Adams. The Trollope Society, mainly consisting of Tory MPs, did not reply. 'They're so grand, one wonders if they've read the books,' said Kathleen Adams. 'On television John Major, a member, gave an impression of Septimus Harding playing the violin. Septimus Harding actually played the cello. It does make you think.' The Arthur Machen Society lost the letter. The society commemorates a writer, one of whose books was described as 'the most acutely and intentionally disagreeable work yet seen in English', and it is the only literary society in which the members are more famous than the man himself. Its president is Barry Humphries, and other members include Carmelite friars, tree surgeons, a Korean called Williams, the man who wrote the music for *The Silence of the Lambs*, and a publisher of comics who, seeking to extend his range of characters, added the Chief Constable of Manchester to them, only to have the Obscene Publications Squad steam in through the front door. With such a membership it is understandable that the secretary mislaid Bill Adams's letter, but it too joined this year.

Some, however, were too deep in shadow, like the Stenbock Society, set up 'for the promotion of the morbid and perverse in literature', also to study the life and works of Eric Stenbock, Estonian count and decadent poet, who is buried in a double grave in Brighton – though only one name, his, is on the headstone. The mighty Brontë Society joined, with its 4,000 members and fifteen paid officers. Twice the size of the next society, the Jane Austen, it even has an education officer whose job it is to attract the young. Most literary societies gave up long ago on the young, but the Brontës, with houses called Wuthering Heights mushrooming in the Tokyo suburbs, can afford a missionary.

At the other end of the spectrum the Thomas Beddoes Society, then with a membership of three, also heeded the call. This had been formed by John Lovell Beddoes, social worker ('somebody has to be'), who had just heard about a kinsman his family had tended to keep secret. 'When he died they brought pressure on his executor not to publish his writings, and I thought, "Hey, I need to find out about this guy." I found he was a Romantic poet who was homosexual and committed suicide at 42. I thought, "Wow, let's have a society." Mr Beddoes, a bearded chap wearing a T-shirt with a portrait of his ancestor, another bearded chap, on the front, and on the back a line of his verse ('If there were dreams to sell, what would you buy?') sketched in the aims of his society. 'If we can give him a boot and get him better known, so much the better.'

He is doing himself an injustice, for his newsletter attracts contributors like Patrick Leigh Fermor, who revealed he had discovered Beddoes in a cave. Amazing characters surface in its pages, such as the poet's father, who invented laughing gas and tried it out on Coleridge, whom he first locked in a box made for him by the scientist Humphrey Davy. As a result he was later put in charge of Coleridge's morphine intake.

'Thomas Lovell Beddoes wasn't on drugs himself,' said his kinsman. 'Mind you, he was on just about everything else.' Membership was now fifty, ten of whom lived overseas, he said, another ten were members of the family, five his own friends, and the rest a hardcore of academics. 'Literary societies have a problem with the academic lot and those who come along for a bit of a laugh,' he added.

Thus while the Robert Louis Stevenson Club announces, 'Seeking Mr Hyde — studies in Robert Louis Stevenson, Symbolism, Myth, and the Pre-modern', a member of the Mary Webb Society said that her membership was a nice way of seeing Shropshire. They had had problems with members getting lost on tours of Shropshire, said a society official.

You get a glimpse of the vast purring expertise of the Jane Austen Society from the first sentence of its newsletter. 'The committee has appointed a membership secretary on a part-time basis to oversee the increasingly technical development and maintenance of the database, and to avail the Society of the benefits of Internet entries on the World Wide Web...'. But as I read on, I found something wonderful. The Oxford branch was describing its June programme. 'An expedition, possibly to Bath.'

I kept picking up leaflets and journals. I read of the George Borrow Society, the Barbara Pym Society, the Fanny Burney Society (formed in New Orleans, in a French restaurant), the Edith Nesbit Society, the Leo Walmsley Society... the Leo Walmsley Society? A novelist of the 1930s, praised as few have been. 'A perfect yarn spinner,' wrote Rebecca West. 'I can only say I laid down this book with respectful wonder,' so Sir Arthur Quiller-Couch said. 'A magnificent piece of work,' H.G. Wells. But the world had forgotten Leo Walmsley when his society was formed. Six of the books are back in print now, and they have 200 members reverently visiting every house lived in by the author during his three marriages. 'We all turned up at his house in St John's Wood and the lady had a terrible shock,' said Fred Lane, the secretary. 'There were 30 of us and she'd never heard of Leo Walmsley, but she showed us round. The only thing is, the more successful a society becomes, the more expensive it is to buy his books. The second-hand trade has heard of Leo Walmsley now.'

'You see these little stalls laid out at our meetings,' said Gabriel Woolf, the broadcaster who is the president of the Alliance. 'You pick up books by people you've never heard of, like Leo Walmsley, and suddenly you're hooked.' A reading by Mr Woolf is the high point of many literary society meetings, and this year, with the actress Rosamund Shanks, he was doing a reading of Mary Webb, all coffins and country passion. 'What be the farm to me?' intoned Mr Woolf, tall and urbane, in his best Shropshire. Later he told me, 'If you thought that was over the top, you should have seen what we cut out.' He has also been Dickens, Tennyson, Auden, Saki and Kipling, but for all his gifts there are some writers he will not touch.

'This actor came up to me, a very pale, gentle type, announced he was going to do a one-man show on William Cowper. I tried to be as encouraging as I could but I remember thinking, "Who the hell wants to see Cowper?" I thought no more about it till one morning I opened *The Times* and read that *The Life and Work of William Cowper* had opened in Carlisle. Not a ticket had been sold, but the usherettes, the report said, had heard him through.'

Other men's enthusiasms always come up when members meet. 'If you really want to meet crackpots, join a literary society,' said the Reverend John Waddington-Feather, representing the Brontës. 'The only reason the council sent me was for fear of some of our weirdos coming.'

'I met this woman, lots of teeth and ambition, banging on about Shelley,' said John Lovell Beddoes. 'She runs something called the Shelley International and they meet once a year under his portrait in the National Portrait Gallery. But I lost interest when she told me Thomas Lovell Beddoes had been a woman.' They told me about the Sherlock Holmes Fellowship, which meets to hear lectures on Victorian headgear, and of one lady, a devotee of nature poetry, who so terrified local farmers they did not dare take down a hedge in case a poet had once paused by it.

On the floor speakers came and went, describing their year in literature. The George Eliot Fellowship announced a George Eliot day culminating in a recital on her old piano, also a walk which would take in a school 'once attended for a short time by her brother Isaac'.

An American lady, the founder of the Dymock Poets Society, described a recent collision between literature and Ledbury District Council. Dymock is a small village just outside the town, where in the years before the Great War, Robert Frost and Edward Thomas lived and their friends came to see them. When Ledbury acquired a new housing estate, the council decided to name its streets after the poets. The only thing was, there were seven streets but only six poets, until someone remembered one of them had had a girlfriend called Eleanor Farjeon, also a writer. The Council solemnly debated this and came to the conclusion it was too difficult a name to spell, at which point a television news crew descended on Ledbury with 'Farjeon' written on large placards. They invited passers-by to pronounce it. The impasse ended when a councillor remembered that W.H. Auden had got married in Ledbury

He did not know that Auden was a homosexual, and that bride and groom, their marriage having been to obtain a British passport for her, parted later that day. When the next estate was built, the Council, said the American lady, called all the streets after cider apples.

Peter Ahearne, a member of the Thomas Hardy Society and a coach driver, offered his transport services. Kenneth Oultram, editor of the Alliance's fanzine, informed the meeting that after years of trying to get them interested in literature, the Royal Mail

had finally succumbed. Stamps were appearing which would feature Dracula, Frankenstein and the Hound of the Baskervilles.

Delegates were beginning to steal away. Fanny Burney went, in
the shape of Lucy Magruder, a schoolteacher representing the
Burney Society of America, who was over for a month's holiday,
in which time she would attend a Mrs Gaskell day in Manchester,
visit every parish church associated with Jane Austen, then go on a
German tour 'in the footsteps of Mrs Gaskell'. 'Oh dear, perhaps
I shouldn't be telling you all this,' said Mrs Magruder. 'You're
laughing already.'

The faces looked down from where their partisans had put the
photographs, John Buchan's cleverest-boy-in-the-school face,
Hardy, whom his wife said looked like Dr Crippen, and only one
face was missing, a plump, balding businessman's face with
a beard. 'I've often thought that strange, but there it is,' said
Kathleen Adams. William Shakespeare alone has no society.

Secret Garden, Private Grief

I N THE MIDDLE OF England there is a secret garden. You can pass and not know it is there, the wall around it is so high, the wrought-iron gate in the arch so beautifully made as to be forbidding. When people move to the village of Farthingstone, near Daventry, they assume that whatever lies beyond that gate must belong to someone. Only the gate is never locked.

But even before I opened it, I had seen something else. About 100 yards away there was a seat set so deep into a wall this formed a cave about it. Cut into the seat was, 'Stranger. Whate'er thy land, or creed or race, rest awhile. There is virtue in the place.' It was a creepy sensation, for this was a tiny village with one church, one pub and one small shop, set on a ridge with no main roads near. Like most English villages in the year 2000, none of its population of some 150 was about in the day. What was so special about this place that some distant, and mysterious, agency should direct attention to it? I opened the gate.

A passageway of tall box hedges led to lawns, and beyond the lawns there was on one side a beautiful ironstone building with columns. No doors. This was open to the weather like a shrine, and on the other side of the lawns there were more columns in the same stone, forming a cloistered walkway around a courtyard. The courtyard was also open, this time to the sky. Everything was so quiet, the craft so perfect, that the questions mounted. What was the place? Who had had it built?

There was a metal plate on a bench in the shrine-like building: 'In memory of my daughter Jane, 1972, and my husband Arthur, 1978, who found happiness here.' But behind this, in the building itself, was an inscription cut into a stone niche like some memorial to the Roman dead. The garden, this read, was given to the village by Philip and Georgette Agnew in memory of their daughter Joy, who was just 22 when she died in 1921. The garden was called Joymead. Not the Agnew Garden or Joy's Garden, but that much older word, Joymead.

In the cloisters there was another inscription in another niche, added by the Agnews in memory of their son Ewen, and those others 'who lost their lives in the Great War or died from its consequences'. That last phrase must have been significant, for Ewen, according to the date, died in 1930. There was one other thing, a sundial, there in memory of a grandson, Joy's son, Michael Evans, killed in World War II. All that beauty was becoming overlain by sadness. And it didn't end there.

In Farthingstone church the three lovely stained-glass windows on the south side, commissioned from William Morris's old firm, are in memory of the three dead Agnew children, the third being a girl who had died in infancy. The private grief of one family rolls round and round the village, and at every turn there is this perfect taste.

Who, and what, were they? Artistic, certainly, the quality of these memorials showed that. But where had they lived? The cost suggested it had to be the Big House. However, this was yet another shock as I started to piece the story together, for though the stables had survived, themselves as grand and as big as any manor house, there was no manor house.

But there was once. Called Littlecourt, it had been bought, and greatly altered, by the Agnews in 1899. When the last of them, old Mrs Agnew, died in 1957, the village was startled to learn that the House, around which their own lives had turned, was to be pulled down. This, it was said, was one of the provisions of her late husband's will, that on her death nobody else might go through the unhappiness the family had known there. And the extraordinary thing is, the House was then demolished, an Irish team moving into the village so that in the end not a stone remained.

Such things happen in history. Richard II tore down the palace of Sheen after the death of his first wife, but you do not encounter this extravagance of grief among late-20th century ratepayers. You can just imagine the consternation in the local council offices, an official being confronted by the fact that not only was the House unoccupied, it no longer existed.

I learnt all this from Peter and Sue Stanton, a young couple who moved to Farthingstone ten years ago, and as part of the village's Millennium History researched and wrote an account of the family. 'When we first came I was astonished to find anyone could go into Joymead at any time,' said Peter, a sales rep. 'I had thought it a private place, I didn't know then that it was the village's big secret. But when we started to write about the family we found people knew so little about them. We knocked on every door and managed to get just one picture of Joy, not even one of her wedding, yet all this was just two generations ago.'

The Agnews, they found out, had been part of the family firm which, in the nineteenth century, starting in a small shop selling clocks in Manchester, moved into the fine art business to the point where they negotiated purchases for the National Gallery. It then diverted into print, the Philip Agnew of Farthingstone, that man of grief, being, of all things, the proprietor of the humorous magazine *Punch*. The Stantons wrote to the firm, still in business in Bond Street, and an elderly nephew replied.

He remembered Philip, he wrote, as an extremely serious man, fond of music and so teetotal he would not allow any alcohol advertising in his magazines, which was strange, for his wife was from a family in the wine business in Egypt. As a small boy, the thing that had most impressed him was her fear of thunder, at the slightest approach of which all curtains had to be drawn and the lights put out, 'a rather unnerving experience for a young visitor,' he added dryly.

The Stantons contacted Mohammed Al Fayed, the present owner of *Punch*, who allowed them access to the magazine records. Here they found that Philip's father, Sir William Agnew, had left £1,353,592 on his death. Now, not long before this the great trade union leader Joseph Arch had campaigned for a weekly wage of 12s a week for agricultural labourers. For most of the population of Farthingstone it must have seemed as though the gods had come to the ridge when a family with this kind of wealth turned up.

Mrs Agnew, the Stantons found, had been a poet, contributing Verses descriptive of the Pastoral Beauties of her Northampton-shire home, which must have done wonders for the circulation of *Punch*. She wrote in faded, archaic language, as in this to Mary, Queen of Scots:

Flow down O brooke, o'er flow in meres
And flood thy wintry medes
That Mary of the Many Teares
May know how my heart bleedes.

Which would account for the name Joymead. Mrs Agnew tried to
revive Morris Dancing in Farthingstone, kitting her dancers out in
full Tudor costume: bonnets, baggy breeches, slashed sleeves, the
lot. Under the trees they stare bemusedly out of a yellowing
group photograph.

The family was active in public works, meeting most of the
cost of bringing water to the village, laying on electricity, restor-
ing the church, so that there seemed to be no end to their benevolence. Mr Agnew became a magistrate (though, as his local
newspaper obituary records, 'he was not of the disposition to sit
in judgement upon others and punish them'), and finally High
Sheriff of the county. And, even when their grief came upon
them, they remembered Farthingstone. After Joy's death from
tuberculosis, Philip Agnew gave, with Joymead, enough money to
pay for a resident caretaker, also for a brass band to play once a
fortnight through the summer evenings, and for a village tea to be
held there on each anniversary of the birthday of his daughter
who, as a child, had written, 'In the very heart of England, safe
from the tumults of the world, lies a small village...'.

Her brother Ewen, himself with not long to live, spoke at the
opening of the garden. 'Let (this) be a place where the old and
infirm may spend calm evenings in the sunset of their lives; where
the middle-aged, gazing southwards over this peaceful English
valley, may gather comfort and strength, mental and physical,
against the coming years; where young men and maidens may find
a pleasant trysting-place; where children may gambol from morn

till eve without causing anxiety to their mothers' minds. . .'. It was 1922. The General Strike was just four years away, a post-war depression was gripping agriculture, yet in Farthingstone one of the gods, high-minded and distant, was speaking to nymphs and shepherds in the Arcady his family had created.

That same year they handed down the Rules of the Garden. No-one might cut flowers, beat carpets, allow 'any horse, pony, mule, ass, bull, ox, cow, calf, heifer, steer, sheep, lamb, goat, hog or sow' to enter, or himself deliver 'any public speech, lecture, prayer, sermon, address of any kind'. There would be no animals, no politics, no religion in Eden. 'They sound like instructions from another world,' said Peter Stanton. But what was it like to be one of the nymphs and shepherds, and to live in Farthingstone under such unremitting benevolence? English villages are places of transit as much as any town. Could anyone in Farthingstone remember life under the Agnews?

'I was in the shop the other day and someone said to me, "You must be the oldest woman in the village." I was flabbergasted. You are, you know, when someone says something like that to you. But I think I must be.' Rachel Frost was fourteen in 1939, when she left school to work in the Big House. Mr Agnew was dead, but Mrs Agnew lived on, alone except for the butler, the cook, the houseboy, the head housemaid and underhousemaid, and Rachel, the lowest of all, the kitchenmaid. 'At mealtimes we all used to sit round a table, according to rank.' Rachel's father and uncle worked in the gardens, her mother as a young girl helped with the washing up.

'She thought the world of Miss Joy. "Nelly, where are you?" That was my mother's name, "I'm in the Blue Room." "Quick, I've got some trifle for you." I remember Mr Agnew as a tall man on a horse. We children would salute him, and very gravely he would touch his cap. But by the time I knew Mrs Agnew, she was this little lady living all on her own. Oh, she used to dress terrible, an old sweater tied around her, wearing shoes too big so you could hear her flip-flopping down the corridors. These Hussar officers we had billeted on us, they called her Waltzing Matilda. She was always in black after Miss Joy died, and would never talk to us, just sent instructions for lunch and dinner, though she hardly ate at all.

'I used to find it very strange. I kept finding these white hairs in the combs in Madam's boudoir, but Madam had brown hair. I mentioned this to the butler, and he said that one night I would have to come round late. So I did, and he said I had to be very quiet. We crept up the stairs, he opened a door to the balcony above the Music Room, it was a huge room, and suddenly there was the sound of a piano.

'Madam was playing a grand piano, I hadn't known until then that she could play, and apparently she hadn't since her husband died. But there was someone else playing as well, a Captain Mose-ley, one of the Hussar officers, on another grand piano. I can see it now, it was magical. I was fifteen years old. Everything around them had dust-sheets over it, even the curtains had covers. But it wasn't that. Madam had her hair down. It was long and white and tied in a blue bow, and she looked so beautiful. The hair I knew must have been a wig, though I don't know how she got all that hair up under it.

'She called on our family a few times, but she would never sit on cushions, she had this fear of infection. And when she talked, she spoke ever so quiet. She looked too frail to be alive, a puff of wind could have taken her away. But she had the whole road rerouted, you know, to go round her house. My uncle called it the New Road.'

Having listened to all this as quietly as the young girl had listened to the pianos, I said, ' Could she do that?'

Miss Frost smiled. 'She did it. They had a whole row of cottages pulled down. I know they had others built in their place, but not quite enough, if you take my meaning. Some of the old had to go and live with their children, and one old chap had to go into the workhouse at Daventry. They was heart-broke, some of the old ones. Mr Agnew, he didn't like the allotment sheds, said they spoiled his view. Know what he did? He had trees planted so they hid the sheds, only then there were pigeons in the trees, which ate all the peas in the allotments. They had a whole farmhouse pulled down once, I think that may have had something to do with the view as well.

'Only then they decided to have a lychgate built for the church. To do that they had to get rid of some of the graves, and this chap, he had the pub, he came running to tell my mother, "Nelly, I've just seen something I doubt I shall ever see again." This coffin was open, and there was a lady in it, with hair down to her knees, just bone of course, but the hair was beautiful. And the wind came and blew it all away. But some people hadn't been buried that long. One old lady never went to church again on account of the fact that the Agnews had had her mother dug up. They had the money, and they could do it.

'They did some good things. If someone was ill they sent soup, and when they paid for the electricity they had it laid underground so you couldn't see it in Joymead. Mind you, you could see it everywhere else. I was too late to see the entertaining and the parties. There was never any guests in my time, except when the Hussars came. I remember this chap, the Hon. Verney Cave, he had this hare sent down from Scotland, monstrous great thing it was, hanging in the larder. It had a bowl under it to catch the blood, only after a while this was catching maggots as well.

'The Hussars had their own cook, a corporal. The trouble was, he didn't know how to cook anything, all he could do was tap-dance round the kitchen, singing, "I'm a little prairie flower / Growing wilder every hour. Nobody wants to cultivate me / So I'm as wild as wild can be." So when the Duke of Gloucester came to supper with the officers, the corporal didn't know how to cook the hare.

'The cook, she wouldn't skin it, she kept getting short of breath whenever she came near it, so I had to do it. She kept prodding me with a rolling pin towards the thing. Not that it needed skinning, when you pulled, whole bits fell off. But we cooked it and made some sort of gravy, and the corporal who served it said he'd seen maggots floating in the gravy. But they ate it. They ate the Gorgonzola as well, and that was even more far gone than the hare. They made a hollow in the cheese, and poured port in and, according to the corporal, you could see the maggots swimming round in circles like they were having a race. The Duke of Gloucester said it was the best meal he'd ever had.'

She paused. 'It was sad for Madam at the end. She had just one servant, and Mr Michael's old nanny used to come and stay, but no one else ever did in that huge house. Still, we had no idea it was going to be pulled down. And the saddest thing of all was still to come. There'd been this huge clearance sale, and my cousin Charlie, he went to Banbury the day after. And I shall never forget this, he said the Agnew photograph albums, and their papers and letters, were blowing all over the Cattle Market. Apparently nobody had emptied the drawers and the cupboards and the deal-ers had just tipped the lot out. That was terrible. Charlie said it was a heartbreaking thing to see.'

It would be hard for any of us to understand how he felt, for this was the family from the Big House, of Miss Joy and Master Ewen, and little Mrs Agnew who feared thunder and cushions but who could still divert roads. All their lives they had been in such awe of them, and now all that was left was blowing round a cattle market.

Peter Stanton is Chairman of the Joymead Managers now. 'A glorified caretaker really, when you think they used to meet on Tuesday afternoons. Who could afford to meet on Tuesday afternoons now?' The Agnew endowment barely covers the annual insurance cost, and no brass bands play on summer evenings. 'And who'd come to listen if they did?'

But they still hold the annual tea on each anniversary of Joy's birthday, and in a good year perhaps half the village comes.

The Last of Things

The Gallows Humorist

I ONLY SPOKE TO HIM a month ago, so it was a shock to hear about the death of Syd Dernley of Mansfield. I can remember as though it were yesterday, and always will, the afternoon six years ago when we met, and Mr Dernley in the neat little bungalow talked about his old job, while Mrs Dernley made scones for us. She kept emerging with fresh batches, chiding me for my lack of appetite, while her husband, brisk and informative, produced a length of rope for my inspection, or sat, lost in nostalgia. And believe me, if there is anything more terrifying than a hangman, it is a nostalgic hangman... Mr Dernley was Britain's last surviving executioner; he was 73.

We met because he took exception to something I had written about a hangman my grandfather knew, who had decorated his front room with nooses and portraits of his Victorian colleagues, and whose life, the *Carmarthen Journal* noted in its 1901 obituary, had been dominated by just one thing, 'a deep-seated longing to participate in the infliction of capital punishment everywhere'.

The paper had begun the obituary with a remarkable sentence: 'He has at last "shot his bolt", as he himself would put it.'

His name was Robert Evans (though on occasion he called himself Anderson), a solicitor's son from Carmarthen, who, by a bizarre coincidence, lived in a house that has subsequently become a symbol of lost innocence to generations of Eng. Lit. graduates: Dylan Thomas's Fern Hill. The hangmen Calcraft and Marwood were his guests here, and successive Home Secretaries must have groaned at seeing that address on the eager letters of advice on scaffold etiquette they received from it most months. 'The doomed one should be addressed firmly and, as far as can be, cheerfully assured that he will not be hurried into eternity without being allowed proper time and means to prepare himself, and he should be made to feel confident that no unnecessary punishment be inflicted on him...'.

Evans or Anderson built a gallows in his garden, on which he would sit his neighbours, my grandfather probably among them, and ply them with strong drink. When I wrote about him I made the point that he would have been none the worse for some urgent medical attention; and in the post a few days later there was a letter. Why, enquired the writer, should a hangman not have a sense of humour? He himself had been a hangman, and he had a sense of humour. Mr Dernley asked me to tea.

But writing about 'Y Crogwr' (The Hangman), safely tucked away in Victorian Wales, or reading about such men in Thomas Hardy, was worlds away from this jolly man hopelessly addicted to practical jokes. At one point he produced a safety razor stuck into one of the old round-socket electric plugs ('Know where I can get this fixed?'), and a little later, a wobbly, lifesized rubber hand which he had in his sleeve ('Shake'). Had it not been for the friendly presence of Mrs Dernley, and my own curiosity, I should have run howling into the spring afternoon in the first minutes of that meeting.

Syd Dernley was in his late sixties then, a good-looking man with wavy hair, who could have been anybody's grandfather with his pipe and cardigan and slippers. Indeed, he was somebody's grandfather, and must have been that somebody's despair with his practical jokes. This man, between the years 1948 and 1953, took part in 28 hangings. I had to keep reminding myself that here was the last living practitioner of something the Anglo-Saxons had brought with them out of the forests. Abolition was not even 25 years old, yet it felt as though I was sitting in a room with Jack Ketch.

At the time Syd Dernley did not want his name used, even though (he gave a leer) it might be worth it just for the shock it would give her next door. But he still felt the shadow of the Home Office on him, which had treated its hangmen like jobbing gardeners, paying them half their fee on the morning after an execution and half a fortnight later, to ensure they did not gossip. The Civil Service was also determined such a man would never achieve the social cachet of his French equivalent, Monsieur de Paris, as he was called, who was a sub-contractor and owned the guillotine, which meant he could supplement his income by showing tourists over the thing. However, the third generation of the Sanson family, whose grandfather had briskly decapitated royalty, was so unnerved by young English women tourists, who not only wanted to see the thing but to pose grinning under the knife, that he took to drink and pawned the French guillotine, thus creating chaos in the French judicial system.

Syd Dernley recalled that his own fee per execution was just three guineas, although later this was raised to five; there were perhaps eight executions in a good year, and travel warrants were

always third-class, although his chief, Albert Pierrepoint, travelled
first. Someone in the Home Office had decided that an assistant
hangman was not a gentleman. Even so, the job was never advertised. Syd Dernley himself applied for it, in hope, as he told me,
of meeting criminals. He was a miner who had an obsession with
the books of Edgar Wallace ('Wrote 123 books, he did, and I've
got 80 of them. It were all Edgar Wallace's fault'). Unfortunately,
Wallace forgot to mention one small fact that might have made all
the difference: the average length of time between the moment the
hangman entered the cell and the moment the trap fell was eight
seconds. It was the best-kept secret that there was always a locked
door, which, if a prisoner inquired about, he was told was a store
for old furniture. Beyond that, just 15 feet beyond it, was the
gallows. Mr Dernley never did get to meet criminals socially.

'If he were honest...'. His wife had brought in another plate
of scones. '...If he were honest, he did it just to get out of the
colliery.'

The Home Office replied with brevity, telling him no vacancy
then existed, but a year later wrote again, just as briefly, requesting
him to present himself for interview at Lincoln jail. 'Governor
were a tall bloke, and he wanted to know my hobbies. I said I
liked shooting. Where did I shoot? Up at Castle. He were a bit
taken aback at that, and asked, did I shoot with the Duke then?
No, I said. I generally shot after Duke had gone to bed. That were
it really. He was so tickled he called the doctor in. "Got a poacher
here, says he wants to be a hangman."'

There followed something so bizarre no black comedy could
hope to match it: the Class of '48 – Syd Dernley and three others
– was sent on a week's training course to Pentonville Prison. Of
his colleagues, Dernley remembers two: a mathematician from ICI
('He were just interested in the mathematics of hanging') and an

ice-cream salesman from Birmingham. *They spent the week in the Condemned Cell, doing long-division sums.* 'You divided 1,000 by the man's weight. What for? For the length of the drop.' Sum after sum, scribbling and puzzling, puzzling and scribbling ('Important that, you get yer sums wrong and you can take a man's head clean off'). They hoped to have Pierrepoint as a tutor, but it was an elderly warder. The practical aspects they tried out on each other, the pinioning and the strapping, and took turns on the lever ('Push forward, just as in a signal box').

No knots. 'The noose is already there.' He had dropped his voice to a whisper. 'Hang on, I think I've still got one about the place somewhere.' What? My host had skipped lightly past me to a drawer in a sideboard, from which he produced a length of rope, the inside of which was bound in leather ('to stop rope burns, that') and one end of which had a metal loop, through which he passed the rope. 'Just a souvenir,' he told me.

I was beyond questions as he told me of the time the four of them attended their first execution at Shrewsbury jail. He had a photograph of them with Pierrepoint, taken outside the railway station, and it could be any works outing, except that after it was over there were three. 'The maths chap, he wet himself in the taxi and emigrated. But me, I was impressed. The clock struck nine, Pierrepoint and his assistant went into the cell and, as I told you, eight seconds later it were all over. Mind you, me and him got it down to seven when we hanged James Inglis who'd murdered a prostitute in Hull. Fastest hanging ever, that. And what's more, the condemned man has no time to be frightened. People talk about the electric chair, but that's cruelty. They talk about the guillotine; that's quick, but it's a bloody mess. Here, I've got one of them as well, made it me-self.' And from somewhere the extraordinary being had produced a tiny working model with a little blade which he pulled up and released. Click. 'But hanging's humane. I timed it from the time that clock in Shrewsbury struck nine. Eight seconds.'

'Perhaps you find this shocking,' murmured Mrs Dernley.

'Nothing shocking about it,' said her husband, before I had time to say anything. 'I'd come home, and the wife would say: "All right". That were all. It were an accepted way of life, and we both believed it had to be done. Of course I tried to keep it secret at first, but we weren't on phone, and the old postmaster had to come puffing up the hill whenever a telegram announced a reprieve. So it was suggested we had a phone put in, only there were a two year waiting list, so then I had to say what me other job were. We had the thing in two days. But, being I were a miner, we lived in a Coal Board house, and the phone people must have had to install an extra pole or something, so they got in touch with the pit manager. He told his clerk, and after that it were like dropping a stone in a puddle.

'For six months there was a hush every time I went in a pub. But after that it were all right. Some of the men even made jokes about it when we were playing dominoes: "Whose drop is it?" "I dunno, ask 'im. 'E's the expert". But nobody said anything adverse, and I've never regretted it. It were a very interesting time in my life, when I got to see a lot of the country and met some people I should never have met in pit.'

But one of the others had regrets. News of the ice-cream salesman's other job leaked out in Birmingham and affected sales to the point where one day his boss called him in. 'Harry, ice-cream and hanging, they don't mix, boy.' Which left two of the Class of '48, though the maddening thing was that Syd Dernley had forgotten what became of the other man. He himself went his busy way, helping to hang Timothy Evans, of whose guilt he remained convinced, as you might expect, for even hangmen aspire to sleep at nights.

At one point I hesitantly touched on the more lurid aspects of folklore, but he was not in the least embarrassed. No, he said, he had never seen hanged men with erections, and it had been part of his job to undress the corpses in the execution pit. Pierrepoint in his autobiography talks of this as a moment of intimacy, where it was just him and 'the poor broken body' of his victim. The last thing he wanted on the gallows was gallows humour, and the day inevitably came when Syd Dernley cracked a joke. Through the post the letter came, brief as the first, informing him there would be no further need of his services.

He felt the disappointment keenly, which was why, for old time's sake, he told me, he had bought a gallows. He bought it off a doctor who had it out of the old Cambridge jail, and it came in a Pickford's van. He sprang to his feet again, and rummaged in that drawer out of which by now I was convinced anything might come. He showed me a photograph of the gallows which he installed in his cellar, with two green spotlights trained on a tailor's dummy he had got from John Collier's. This had come without a head, so he had arranged a white bust on its shoulders — at which I started, for there was something familiar about that gaunt profile.

'Hey, that's Dante you're hanging.'

'Who?'

'Dante. Italian poet.'

'That's who it is? I often wondered. Doctor threw it in when I bought gallows.' His cellar was not high enough for this to be assembled with the drop beneath it, so he put two blocks of wood under the thing, just enough, he smiled, just enough for the trap to creak. Those were social years. 'Word got round, and all sorts turned up. A managing director came. "I understand you have a gallows in your cellar." I took him down. "I understand you have a rope." He stood there. "Excuse me, may I have the rope round my neck?"'

It was like those cosy afternoons long ago, chez Sanson all over again, but the experience did not lead Mr Dernley to booze. He took flashlit photographs and had certificates printed, some of which his victims framed and hung on their walls. He was keeping a post office then, and time passed merrily enough until, his wife being taken ill, her cousin came to keep house for him, who, of course, did not know where anything was.

One morning, a man came to read the electric meters. Syd Dernley was busy in his post office, but he noticed the man walk up his garden path. Five minutes later he saw the man come running down it, running faster than he had ever seen any man run, down the path and up the street till he was lost to sight Which was odd, considering he had come by car.

His wife's cousin had not known where the meters were, so the man had said to leave it to him, and had opened a few cupboard doors before opening the one leading down into the cellar. He must have switched the lights on, at which point the two green spots came on. 'You know, I can't remember anyone coming to read our meters after that. It were all estimates.'

At the time I was writing a column for the *Sunday Express* and thought hangman Syd an ideal profile for the paper. But no, they wouldn't touch it with a bargepole; it was explained to me that however much the paper's readers might approve of hanging, it would be too much of a shock to confront them with a hangman. Their ancestors were not so squeamish. Hangmen, along with their victims, were the first authentic working-class heroes (and hangmen had a longer shelf life). Crowds met them when they arrived on business in county towns, and newspapers scrupulously noted their taste in dress. 'Mr Berry,' recorded the *Carmarthen Journal*, '*unostentatiously* dressed in a plain suit of dark clothing and wearing a red Turkish fez.' (The italics are mine.)

I kept in touch with Syd Dernley, a helpful man, who at one point sent me a table of weights and drops, a sort of hangman's ready-reckoner. He also sent me various ideas for feature articles.

In return, I read and tried to help him with a memoir he had written about his poaching days, and I must have kept this for some time, as I remember an irritated reminder from him ('If you don't want to find yourself dangling from one of your apple trees'). I never could cope with his humour.

When we spoke last month, he told me the last gallows of all had finally been taken down ('You know, the one they had at Wandsworth for blokes with a mind to run off with Queen'), although it had subsequently been reassembled at the Prison Officers' Museum near Rugby. He urged me to go and see it; he himself, he said, had already been twice.

End of an Era

THE HOUSE IS up for sale. I have the particulars in front of me, and I am staring with admiration at one phrase, 'situated in well-wooded grounds'. You have to hand it to estate agents: if Tarzan's house came on the market, that too would be in well-wooded grounds.

Every time he called, said the man from the village, he felt more and more like the Prince hacking his way through to Sleeping Beauty. But when it came to the actual building even the estate agents gave up. Undergrowth they could cope with, but this was beyond their adaptable little adjectives. It was, said the prospectus lamely, 'an interesting residence'.

The house had fascinated me ever since I moved to the village five years ago. It stood, or rather lurked, in its wood, quite alone and beyond the street lamps, 200 yards from the last houses, at the top of a small hill. At first I thought it was empty, for though you could see where a drive had been, the brambles and grass had closed in until there was little more than a sheep track leading from the gate. There were no signs of life, and at night the lights were never on.

But then there was no need for lights. Its owner had been totally blind for the last 20 years of her life. She was the vicar's daughter and had lived there ever since her father died in the 1930s. At that point her grandmother, who had never been able to stand clergymen, came back into her life to buy the land and build the house. Only the old lady built it in this crazy style, half suburban villa, with brick and rendering, and half Tudor. All the windows were latticed and all the interior doors were without metal fittings, just massive wooden latches.

The gardens went first, because of the cost of the upkeep. The grass tennis court under the trees became a lawn, and then the lawn went and there was just undergrowth. The greenhouse was abandoned, and the sheds left locked. When the auctioneer's men finally came they had to fell trees just to get to the garage.

The older villagers, who remembered the vicar's daughter as a young woman riding her bicycle erratically down the hill, kept an eye on her, but the majority, the newcomers, did not even know of her existence. She was ferried like royalty from her house to church and the odd tea party; the village shop delivered her groceries. Just outside the front door was a tiny hutch where she kept her one hen; daily she must have groped her way to that, and the one egg.

When I was first told about her I remember thinking that I would probably never come on anything like this again, a community, not its social services or its nurses, but people who had known her looking after one of their own, as their ancestors would have done. The blind lady in the wood was one of the village's last links with its history.

She was ill for just three weeks and went into hospital, asking one of the villagers to keep an eye on the house for her, but she did not return. She died, as she had lived, without causing trouble to anyone.

And now her house is up for sale. For weeks people have come and gone; gouging into the window sills with penknives, hacking pieces out of the plaster, the way house-hunters do now. Soon someone else will be there, felling the trees, cutting a path, painting the beams white. They may frighten truculent children with tales of the old lady in the wood.

I drove past on the day of her death, and on the gate someone had left a single red rose.

A Ghost in the Church

A SMALL CHURCH IS TO CLOSE. There were a few paragraphs in the local paper, but it is the usual matter of accountancy, a congregation of nine unable to afford repair bills of £150,000. But this is no ordinary church – this is St Guthlac's at Passenham in Northamptonshire. Come inside for a moment.

It is a summer evening and there are shadows on the two inscriptions above the south door. Both are in Latin. The first celebrates the rebuilding of the chancel in 1626, and the text is what you would expect. Psalm 116, verse 12. 'How can I repay the Lord for his goodness to me?' But the second text is not at all what you would expect. St Luke 12, verse 20, *Stulte Hoc Nocte*... 'You fool, this very night your life will be demanded of you.'

The church guide-book, its words chosen with care, describes this as an enigma in its context. It does not mention the story, still told, that when the man who had the chancel rebuilt came to be buried, his bearers heard a known voice speak from the coffin. 'I am not ready.' They opened the coffin but there was no movement in the wild, spade-bearded face, which now, in marble, is also in the chancel wall. Yet when they buried him beside the altar the voice spoke again. 'I am not ready yet.'

And you are in familiar territory, are you not? An English parish church; a puzzling quotation; a dominating long-dead local figure. All you are waiting for is the horror to come as quietly as the tide and break among stone flags and the damp, for in life you have stepped into a ghost story by M.R. James.

Three-and-a-half centuries after his death they still remember Sir Robert Banastre in Passenham, mothers bringing children to order by the mention of his name. Architectural historians also remember him. His chancel, said one, was unique. And it is. Sit down, for the restoration work of the 1950s has restored it to the way it would have looked in Banastre's time. You will have already noticed that you are in an unusual place, entering from the west through the bell tower, past the eighteenth-century boxed pews painted a pale matt green. And then you come to Banastre's chancel.

Even old Pevsner was startled into one of his rare, wintry adjectives. 'Very remarkable furnishings,' he wrote. The roof is a deep blue, sprinkled with gold stars so you feel you have strayed into a planetarium. But everything else is deliberately archaic. On the walls are paintings of biblical figures, not put up to overawe the poor, but huge and elegant. The only thing is, they were put up centuries after the fashion for wall paintings had gone, and just before it became imperative to whitewash them over. The man who had this done must have thought himself in his private chapel, and where St Mark should be, his own face, under a linen skullcap, looks down.

And Sir Robert had only just begun. His choir stalls froth with carvings and there are misericords from a time long after these had gone out of ritual. You sit there, passing your hands over carvings in the twilight, and you have the odd sensation these are moving. So you bend to look, and wish you hadn't. For these are not the quaint beasts of the Middle Ages, these were meant to terrify: hoofed demons, legs shaggy with hair, their mouths agape, eyes bulging, breasts sagging.

Why did he have all this done? It has been suggested Banastre was a secret Catholic, this prominent courtier to James I and Charles I, but no secret Catholic would have dared commission anything like this. And why did his villagers hate him so? The local historian Sir Gordon Roberts thought it might be because Banastre had enclosed their common land, but this, he found, had been done long before. As for the stories of cruelty, he found that Banastre's will bulged with bequests.

Yet they did hate him and went on hating him and told so many ghost stories these have become matter of fact. I asked one man when he had last seen a ghost, and he said Tuesday night, when a voice spoke out of the darkness. A human shape? Oh yes, except this was a human shape in a large hat with a feather.

How odd it should feel so remote here, for the main road is only half a mile away and over the water meadows the roofs of Milton Keynes show above the willow trees, massed like an army. There are just fifteen houses in Passenham, also a tithe barn, the manor, the church. And if it is remote now, think how much more it must have been in the early seventeenth century, when a powerful man might have done what he wanted here.

A summer evening with shadows, and the sudden wish to be elsewhere.

Note: But the church didn't close.